Ancient and Modern Initiation
Max Heindel

Ancient and Modern Initiation

A Cornerstone Book
Published by Cornerstone Book Publishers
An Imprint of Michael Poll Publishing
Copyright © 2007 and 2013 by Cornerstone Book Publishers

First Cornerstone Edition 2007
Second Cornerstone Edition 2013

Cornerstone Book Publishers
New Orleans, LA

www.cornerstonepublishers.com

ISBN: 1613421478
ISBN-13: 978-1-61342-147-5

MADE IN THE USA

TABLE OF CONTENTS

PART I

PART II

Ancient and Modern Initiation

PART ONE

THE TABERNACLE IN THE WILDERNESS

CHAPTER ONE

THE ATLANTEAN MYSTERY TEMPLE

Ever since mankind, the prodigal spirit sons of our Father in Heaven, wandered into the wilderness of the world and fed upon the husks of its pleasures, which starve the body, there has been within man's heart a soundless voice urging him to return; but most men are so engrossed in material interests that they hear it not. The Mystic Mason who has heard this inner voice feels impelled by an inner urge to seek for the Lost Word; to build a house of God, a temple of the spirit, where he may meet the Father face to face and answer His call.

Nor is he dependent upon his own resources in this quest, for our Father in Heaven has Himself prepared a way marked with guide posts which will lead us to Him if we follow. But as we have forgotten the divine Word and would be unable now to comprehend its meaning, the Father speaks to us in the language of symbolism, which both hides and reveals the spiritual truths we must understand before we can come to Him. Just as we give to our children picture books which reveal to their nascent minds intellectual concepts which they could not otherwise understand, so also each God-given symbol has a deep meaning which could not be learned without that symbol.

God is spirit and must be worshipped in spirit. It is therefore strictly forbidden to make a material likeness of Him, for nothing we could make would convey an adequate idea. But as we hail the flag of our country with joy and enthusiasm because it awakens in our breasts the tenderest feelings for home and our loved ones, because it stirs our noblest impulse, because it is a symbol of all the things which we hold dear, so also do different divine symbols which have been given to mankind from time to time speak to that forum of truth which is within our hearts, and awaken our con-

2

sciousness to divine ideas entirely beyond words. Therefore symbolism, which has played an all-important part in our past evolution, is still a prime necessity in our spiritual development; hence the advisability of studying it with our intellects and our hearts.

It is obvious that our mental attitude today depends on how we thought yesterday, also that our present condition and circumstances depend on how we worked or shirked in the past. Every new thought or idea which comes to us we view in the light of our previous experience, and thus we see that our present and future are determined by our previous living. Similarly the path of spiritual endeavor which we have hewn out for ourselves in past existences determines our present attitude and the way we must go to attain our aspirations. Therefore we can gain no true perspective of our future development unless we first familiarize ourselves with the past.

It is in recognition of this fact that modern Masonry harks back to the temple of Solomon. That is very well as far as it goes, but in order to gain the fullest perspective we must also take into consideration the ancient Atlantean Mystery Temple, the Tabernacle in the Wilderness. We must understand the relative importance of that Tabernacle, also of the first and second temples, for there were vital differences between them, each fraught with cosmic significance; and within them all was the foreshadowing of the CROSS, sprinkled with BLOOD, which was turned to ROSES.

THE TABERNACLE IN THE WILDERNESS

We read in the Bible the story of how Noah and a remnant of his people with him were saved from the flood and formed the nucleus of the humanity of the Rainbow Age in which we now live. It is also stated that Moses led his people out of Egypt, the land of the

Bull, Taurus, through waters which engulfed their enemies and set them free as a chosen people to worship the Lamb, Aries, into which sign the sun had then entered by precession of the equinox. These two narratives relate to one and the same incident, namely, the emergence of infant humanity from the doomed continent of Atlantis into the present age of alternating cycles where summer and winter, day and night, ebb and flow, follow each other. As humanity had then just become endowed with mind, they began to realize the loss of the spiritual sight which they had hitherto possessed, and they developed a yearning for the spirit world and their divine guides which remains to this day, for humanity has never ceased to mourn their loss. Therefore the ancient Atlantean Mystery Temple, the Tabernacle in the Wilderness, was given to them that they might meet the Lord when they had qualified themselves by service and subjugation of the lower nature by the Higher Self. Being designed by Jehovah it was the embodiment of great cosmic truths hidden by a veil of symbolism which spoke to the inner or Higher Self.

In the first place it is worthy of notice that this divinely designed Tabernacle was given to a chosen people, who were to build it from freewill offerings given out of the fullness of their hearts. Herein is a particular lesson, for the divine pattern of the path of progress is never given to anyone who has not first made a covenant with God that he will serve Him and is wiling to offer up his heart's blood in a life of service without self-seeking The term "Mason" is derived from PHREE MESSEN, which is an Egyptian term meaning "Children of Light." In the parlance of Masonry, God is spoken of as the Grand Architect. ARCHE is a Greek word which means "Primordial substance." TEKTON is the Greek name for builder. It is said that Joseph, the father of Jesus, was a "CARPENTER," but the Greek word is TEKTON--builder. It is also said that Jesus was a "tekton," a builder. Thus every true mystic Freemason is a child of light according to the divine pattern given him by our Father in Heaven. To this end he dedicates his whole heart, soul, and mind. It is, or should be, his aspiration to be "greatest in the kingdom of God," and therefore he must be THE SERVANT

OF ALL.

The next point which calls for notice is the location of the temple with respect to the cardinal points, and we find that it was laid directly east and west. Thus we see that the path of spiritual progress is the same as the star of empire; it travels from east to west. The aspirant entered at the eastern gate and pursued the path by way of the Altar of Burnt Offerings, the Brazen Laver, and the Holy Place to the westernmost part of the Tabernacle, where the Ark, the greatest symbol of all, was located in the Holy of Holies. As the wise men of the East followed the Christ star westward to Bethlehem, so does the spiritual center of the civilized world shift farther and farther westward, until today the crest of the spiritual wave which started in China on the western shores of the Pacific has now reached the eastern shores of the same ocean, where it is gathering strength to leap once more in its cyclic journey across the waste 'of waters, to recommence in a far future a new cyclic journey around the earth.

The ambulant nature of this Tabernacle in the Wilderness is therefore an excellent symbolical representation of the fact that man is migratory in his nature, an eternal pilgrim, ever passing from the shores of time to eternity and back again. As a planet revolves in its cyclic journey around the primary sun, so man, the little world or microcosm, travels in cyclic circle dance around God, who is the source and goal of all.

The great care and attention to detail regarding the construction of the Tabernacle in the Wilderness shows that something far more exalted than what struck the eye of sense was intended in its construction. Under its earthly and material show there was designed a representation of things heavenly and spiritual such as should be full of instruction to the candidate for Initiation and should not this reflection excite us to seek an intimate and familiar acquaintance with this ancient sanctuary? Surely it becomes us to consider all parts of its plan with serious, careful, and reverential attention, remembering at every step the heavenly origin of it all, and humbly endeavoring to penetrate through the shadows of its earthly service into the sublime and glorious realities which according to the wisdom of the spirit it proposes for our solemn contemplation.

In order that we may gain a proper conception of this sacred place we must consider the Tabernacle itself, its furniture and its court. The illustration opposite page 33 may assist the student to form a better conception of the arrangement within.

THE COURT OF THE TABERNACLE

This was an enclosure which surrounded the Tabernacle. Its length was twice its width, and the gate was at the east end. This gate was enclosed by a curtain of blue, scarlet, and purple fine twined linen, and these colors show us at once the status of this Tabernacle in the Wilderness. We are taught in the sublime gospel of John that "God is Light," and no description or similitude could convey a better conception or one more enlightening to the spiritual mind than these words. When we consider that even the greatest of modern telescopes have failed to find the borders of light, though they penetrate space for millions and millions of miles, it gives us a weak but comprehensive idea of the infinitude of God.

We know that this light, which is God, is refracted into three primary colors by the atmosphere surrounding our earth, viz., blue, yellow, and red; and it is a fact well known to every occultist that the ray of the Father is blue, while that of the Son is yellow, and the color of the Holy Spirit's ray is red. Only the strongest and most spiritual ray can hope to penetrate to the seat of consciousness of the life wave embodied in our mineral kingdom, and therefore we find about the mountain ranges the blue ray of the Father reflected back from the barren hillsides and hanging as a haze over canyons and gulches. The yellow ray of the Son mixed with the blue of the Father gives life and vitality to the plant world, which therefore reflects back a green color, for it is incapable of keeping the ray WITHIN. But in the animal kingdom, to which unregenerate man belongs anatomically, the three rays are absorbed, and that of the Holy Spirit gives the red color to his flesh and blood. The mixture of the blue and the red is evident in the purple blood, poisoned because sinful. But the yellow is never evident until it manifests as a soul body, the golden "WEDDING garment" of the mystic Bride of the mystic Christ evolved from within.

Thus the colors on the veils of the Temple, both at the gate and at the entrance of the Tabernacle, showed that this structure was designed for a period previous to the time of Christ, for it had only the blue and the scarlet colors of the Father and the Holy Spirit together with their mixture, purple. But white is the synthesis of all colors, and therefore the yellow Christ ray was hidden in that part of the veil until in the fullness of time Christ should appear to emancipate us from the ordinances that bind, and initiate us into the full liberty of Sons of God, Sons of Light, Children of Light, Phree Messen or Mystic Masons.

CHAPTER TWO

THE BRAZEN ALTAR AND LAVER

THE BRAZEN ALTAR was placed just inside the eastern gate, and it was used for the sacrifice of animals during the temple service. The idea of using bulls and goats as sacrifices seems barbaric to the modern mind, and we cannot realize that they could ever have had any efficacy in that respect. The Bible does indeed bear out this view of the matter, for we are told repeatedly that God desires not sacrifice but a broken spirit and a contrite heart, and that He has no pleasure in sacrifices of blood. In view of this fact it seems strange that sacrifices should ever have been commanded. But we must realize that no religion can elevate those whom it is designed to help if its teachings are too far above their intellectual or moral level. To appeal to a barbarian, religion must have certain barbaric traits. A religion of love could not have appealed to those people, therefore they were given a law which demanded "an eye for an eye, and a tooth for a tooth." There is not in the Old Testament any mention whatever of immortality, for these people could not have understood a heaven nor aspired to it. But they loved material possessions, and therefore they were told that if they did right they and their seed should dwell in the land forever, that their cattle should be multiplied, et cetera.

They loved material possessions, and they knew that the increases of the flock were due to the Lord's favor and given by Him for merit. Thus they were taught to do right in the hope of a reward in this present world. They were also deterred from wrongdoing by the swift punishment which was meted out to them in retribution for their sins. This was the only way to reach them. They could not have done right for the sake of right, nor could they have understood the principle of making themselves "living sacrifices," and they probably felt the loss of an animal for sin as we would feel the pangs of conscience because of wrongdoing.

The Altar was made of brass, a metal not found in nature, but made by man from copper and zinc. Thus it is symbolically shown that sin was not originally contemplated in our scheme of evolution and is an anomaly in nature as well as its consequences, pain and death, symbolized by the sacrificial victims. But while the Altar itself was made from metals artificially compounded, the fire which burned thereon unceasingly was of divine origin, and it was kept alive from year to year with the most jealous care. No other fire was ever used, and we may note with profit that when two presumptuous and rebellious priests dared to disregard this command and use strange fire, they met with an awful retribution and instant death. When we have once taken the oath of allegiance to the mystic Master, the HIGHER SELF, it is extremely dangerous to disregard the precepts then given.

When the candidate appears at the eastern gate he is "poor, naked, and blind." He is at that moment an object of charity, needing to be clothed and brought to the light, but this cannot be done at once in the mystic Temple.

During the time of his progress from the condition of nakedness until he has been clothed in the gorgeous robes of the high priest there is a long and difficult path to be traveled. The first lesson which he is taught is that man advances by sacrifices alone. In the Christian Mystic Initiation when the Christ washes the feet of His disciples, the explanation is given that unless the minerals decomposed and were offered us as embodiments for the plant kingdom, we should have no vegetation; also, did not the plant food furnish sustenance for the animals, these latter beings could not find expression; and so on, the higher is always feeding on the lower. Therefore man has a duty to them, and so the Master washes the feet of His disciples symbolically performing for them the menial service as recognition of the fact that they have served Him as stepping-stones to something higher.

Similarly, when the candidate is brought to the Brazen Altar, he learns the lesson that the animal is sacrificed for his sake, giving its body for food and its skin for clothing. Moreover, he sees the dense cloud of smoke hovering over the Altar and perceives within it a light, but that light is too dim, too much enshrouded in smoke, to be of permanent guidance to him. His spiritual eyes are weak, however, and it would not do to expose them at once to the light of greater spiritual truths.

We are told by the apostle Paul that the Tabernacle in the Wilderness was a shadow of greater things to come. It may therefore be of interest and profit to see what is the meaning of this Brazen Altar, with its sacrifices and burning flesh, to the candidate who comes to the Temple in modern times. In order that we may understand this mystery, we must first grasp the one great and absolutely essential idea which underlies all true mysticism, viz., that these things are WITHIN and not without. Angelus Silesius says about the Cross:

"Though Christ a thousand times in Bethlehem be born,
And not within thyself thy soul will be forlorn.
The Cross on Golgotha thou lookest to in vain,
Unless within thyself it be set up again."

This idea must be applied to every symbol and phase of mystic experience. It is not the Christ without that saves, but THE CHRIST WITHIN. The Tabernacle was built at one time; it is clearly seen in the Memory of Nature when the interior sight has been developed to a sufficient degree; but no one is ever helped by the outward symbol. We must build the Tabernacle within our own hearts and consciousness. We must live through, as an actual inner experience, the whole ritual of service there. We must become both the Altar of sacrifice and the sacrificial animal lying upon it. We must become both the priest that slays the animal and the animal that is slain. Later we must learn to identify ourselves with the mystic Laver, and we must learn to wash therein in spirit. Then we must enter behind the first veil, minister in the East Room, and so on through the whole Temple service till we BECOME the greatest of all these ancient symbols, the Shekinah Glory, or it will avail us nothing. In short, before the symbol of the Tabernacle can really help us, we must transfer it from the wilderness of space to a home in our hearts so that when we have become everything that that symbol is, we shall also have become that which it stands for spiritually.

Let us then commence to build within ourselves the Altar of sacrifice, first that we may offer upon it our wrongdoings and then expiate them in the crucible of remorse. This is done under the modern system of preparation for discipleship by an exercise performed in the evening and scientifically designed by the Hierophants of the Western Mystery School for the advancement of the aspirant on the path which leads to discipleship. Other schools have given a similar exercise, but this one differs in one particular point from all previous methods. After explaining the exercises we shall also give the reason for this great and cardinal difference. This special method has such a far-reaching effect that it enables one to learn now not only the lessons which one should ordinarily learn in this life, but also attain a development which otherwise could not be reached until future lives.

After retiring for the night the body is relaxed. This is very important, for when any part of the body is tense, the blood does not circulate unimpeded; part of it is temporarily imprisoned under pressure. As all spiritual development depends upon the blood, the maximum effort to attain soul growth cannot be made when any part of the body is in tension.

When perfect relaxation has been accomplished, the aspirant to the higher life begins to review the scenes of the day, but he does not start with the occurrences of the morning and finish with the events of the evening. He views them in REVERSE order: first the scenes of the evening, then the events of the afternoon, and lastly the occurrences of the morning. The reason for this is that from the moment of birth when the child draws its first complete breath, the air which is inspired into the lungs carries with it a picture of the outside world, and as the blood courses through the left ventricle of the heart, each scene of life is pictured upon a minute atom located there. Every breath brings with it new pictures, and thus there is engraved upon that little seed atom a record of every scene and act in our whole life from the first breath to the last dying gasp. After death these pictures from the basis of our purgatorial existence. Under the conditions of the spirit world we suffer pangs of conscience so acute that they are unbelievable for every evil deed we have done, and we are thus discouraged from continuing on the path of wrongdoing. The intensity of the joys which we experience on account of our good deeds acts as a goad to spur us on the path of virtue in future lives. But in the post-mortem existence this panorama of life is reenacted in reverse order for the purpose of showing first the effects and then the causes which generated them that the spirit may learn how the law of cause and effect operates in life. Therefore the aspirant who is under the scientific guidance of the Elder Brothers of the Rosicrucians is taught to perform his evening exercise also in reverse order and to judge himself each day that he may escape the purgatorial suffering after death. But let it be understood that no mere perfunctory review of the scenes of the day will avail. It is not enough when we come to a scene where we have grievously wronged somebody that we just say, "Well, I feel rather sorry that I did it. I wish I had not done it." At that time we are the sacrificial animal lying upon the Alter of Burnt Offerings, and unless we can feel in our hearts the divinely enkindled fire of remorse burn to the very marrow of our bones because of our wrongdoings during the day, we are not accomplishing anything.

During the ancient dispensation all the sacrifices were rubbed with salt before being placed upon the Altar of Burnt Offerings. We all know how it smarts and burns when we accidentally rub salt into a fresh wound. This rubbing of salt into the sacrifices in that ancient Mystery Temple symbolized the intensity of the burning which we must feel when we as living sacrifices place ourselves upon the Altar of Burnt Offerings. It is the feeling of remorse, of deep and sincere sorrow for what we have done, which eradicates the picture from the seed atom and leaves it clean and stainless, so that as under the ancient dispensation transgressors were justified when they brought to the Altar of Burnt Offerings a sacrifice which was there burnt, so we in modern times by scientifically performing the evening exercise of retrospection wipe away the record of our sins. It is a foregone conclusion that we cannot continue evening after evening to perform this living sacrifice without becoming better in consequence and ceasing, little by little, to do the things for which we are forced to blame ourselves when we have retired for the night. Thus, in addition to cleansing us from our faults this exercise elevates us to a higher level of spirituality than we could otherwise reach in the present life.

It is also noteworthy that when anyone had committed a grievous crime and fled to the sanctuary, he found safety in the shadow of the Altar of sacrifice, for there only the divinely enkindled fire could execute judgment. He escaped the hands of man by putting himself under the hand of God. Similarly also, the aspirant who acknowledges his wrongdoing nightly by fleeing to the altar of living judgment thereby obtains sanctuary from the law of cause and effect, and "though his sins be as scarlet they shall be white as snow."

THE BRAZEN LAVER

The Brazen laver was a large basin which was always kept full of water. It is said in the Bible that it was carried on the backs of twelve oxen, also made of brass, and we are told that their hind parts were toward the center of the vessel. It appears from the Memory of Nature, however, that those animals were not oxen but symbolical representations of the twelve signs of the zodiac. Humanity was at that time divided into twelve groups, one group for each zodiacal sign. Each symbolic animal attracted a particular ray, and as the holy water used today in Catholic churches is magnetized by the priest during the ceremony of consecration, so also the water in this Laver was magnetized by the divine Hierarchies who guided humanity.

There can be no doubt concerning the power of holy water prepared by a strong and magnetic personality. It takes on or absorbs the effluvia from his vital body, and the people who use it become amenable to his rule in a degree commensurate to their sensitiveness. Consequently the Brazen Lavers in the ancient Atlantean mystery Temples, where the water was magnetized by divine Hierarchs of immeasurable power, were a potent factor in guiding the people in accordance with the wishes of these ruling powers. Thus the priests were in perfect subjection to the mandates and dictates of their unseen spiritual leaders, and through them the people were made to follow blindly. It was required of the priests that they wash their hands and feet before going into the Tabernacle proper. If this command was not obeyed, death would follow immediately on the priest entering into the Tabernacle. We may therefore say that as the keyword of the Brazen Altar was "justification" so the central idea of the Brazen Laver was "consecration."

"Many are called but few are chosen." We have the example of the rich young man who came to Christ asking what he must do to be perfect. He asserted that he had kept the law, but when Christ gave the command, "Follow me," he could not, for he had many riches which held him fast as in a vise. Like the great majority he was content if he could only escape condemnation, and like them he was too lukewarm to strive for commendation merited by service. The Brazen Laver is the symbol of sanctification and consecration of the life to service. As Christ entered upon His three years' ministry through the baptismal waters, so the aspirant to service in the ancient Temple must sanctify himself in the sacred stream which must sanctify himself in the sacred stream which flowed from the Molten Sea. And the mystic Mason endeavoring

14

to build a temple "without sound of hammer" and to serve therein must also consecrate himself and sanctify himself. He must be willing to give up all earthly possessions that he may follow the CHRIST WITHIN. Though he may retain his material possessions he must regard them as a sacred trust to be used by him as a wise steward would use his master's possessions. And we must be ready in everything to obey this Christ within when he says, "Follow me," even though the shadow of the Cross looms darkly at the end, for without this utter abandonment of the life to the Light, to the higher purposes, there can be no progress. Even as the Spirit descended upon Jesus when he arose from the baptismal water of consecration, so also the mystic Mason who bathes in the Laver of the Molten Sea begins dimly to hear the voice of the Master within his own heart teaching him the secrets of the Craft that he may use them for the benefit of others.

CHAPTER THREE

EAST ROOM OF THE TEMPLE

HAVING MOUNTED the first steps upon the path the aspirant stands in front of the veil which hangs before the mystic Temple. Drawing this aside he enters into the East Room of the sanctuary, which was called the HOLY PLACE. No window or opening of any sort was provided in the Tabernacle to let in the light of day, but this room was never dark. Night and day it was brightly illuminated by burning lamps.

Its furniture was symbolical of the methods whereby the aspirant may make SOUL GROWTH BY SERVICE. It consisted of three principal articles: The ALTER OF INCENSE, the TABLE OF SHEWBREAD, and the GOLDEN CANDLESTICK from which the light proceeded.

It was not allowable for the common Israelite to enter this sacred apartment and behold the furniture. No one but a priest might pass the outer veil and go in even as far as this first room. The Golden Candlestick was placed on the south side of the Holy Place so as to be to the left of any person who stood in the middle of the room. It was made entirely of pure gold, and consisted of a shaft or principal stem, rising upright from a base, together with six branches. These branches started at three different points on the stem and curved upward in three partial circles of varying diameter, symbolizing the three periods of development (Saturn, Sun, and Moon Periods) which man went through before the Earth period, which was not half spent. This latter period was signified by the seventh light. Each of these seven branches terminated in a lamp, and these lamps were supplied with the purest olive oil, which was made by a special process. The priests were required to take care that the Candlestick was never without a light. Every day the lamps were examined, dressed, and supplied with oil so that they might burn perpetually.

The TABLE OF SHEWBREAD was placed on the north side of the apartment so as to be in THE RIGHT HAND of the priest when he walked up toward the second veil. Twelve loaves of unleavened bread were continually kept upon this table. They were placed in two piles, one loaf upon another, and on top of each pile there was a small quantity of frankincense. These loaves were called shewbread, or bread of the face, because they were set solemnly forth before the presence of the Lord, who dwelt in the Shekinah Glory behind the second veil. Every Sabbath day these loaves were changed by the priests, the old ones being taken away and new ones put in their place. The bread that was taken away was used by the priests to eat, and no one else was allowed to taste it; neither were they suffered to eat it anywhere except within the Court of the Sanctuary, because it was most holy, and therefore might only be taken by sacred persons upon holy ground. THE INCENSE THAT WAS UPON THE TWO PILES OF SHEW-BREAD WAS BURNED when the bread was changed, as an offering by fire unto the Lord, as a memorial instead of the bread.

The ALTAR OF INCENSE or the Golden Altar was the third article of furniture in the East Room of the Temple. It was situated in the center of the room, that is to say, halfway between the north and the south walls, in front of the second veil. No flesh was ever burned upon this Altar, nor was it ever touched with blood except on the most solemn occasions, and then its horns alone were marked with the crimson stain. The smoke that arose from its top was never any other than the smoke of burning incense. This went up every morning and evening, filling the sanctuary with a fragrant cloud and sending a refreshing odor out through all the courts and far over the country on every side for miles beyond. Because incense was thus burned every day it was called "A PERPETUAL INCENSE before the Lord."

It was not simple frankincense which was burned, but a compound of this with other sweet spices, made according to the direction of Jehovah for this special purpose and so considered holy, such as no man was allowed to make like unto for common use. THE PRIEST WAS CHARGED NEVER TO OFFER STRANGE INCENSE on the Golden Altar, that is, any other than the sacred composition. This Altar was placed directly before the veil on the outside of it, but before the Mercy Seat, which was within the second veil; for though he that ministered at the Altar of Incense could not see the Mercy Seat because of the interposing veil, yet he must look toward it and direct his incense that way. And it was customary when the cloud of fragrant incense rose above the temple for all the people who were standing without in the Court of the Sanctuary to send up their prayers to God, each one silently by himself.

THE MYSTIC SIGNIFICANCE OF THE EAST ROOM AND ITS FURNITURE

THE GOLDEN CANDLESTICK

As previously said, when the priest stood in the center of the East Room of the Tabernacle, the Seven-branched Candlestick was ON HIS LEFT toward the SOUTH. This was symbolical of the fact that the seven light-givers or planets which tread the mystic circle dance around the central orb, the sun, travel in the narrow belt comprising eight degrees on either side of the sun's path, which is called the zodiac. "God is Light," and the "Seven Spirits before the Throne" are God's ministers; therefore THEY ARE MESSENGERS OF LIGHT to humanity. Furthermore, as the heavens are ablaze with light when the moon in its phases arrives at the "full" in the eastern part of the heavens, so also the East Room of the Tabernacle was filled with LIGHT, indicating VISIBLY the presence there of God and His seven Ministers, the STAR ANGELS.

We may note, in passing, the light of the Golden Candlestick, which was clear and the flame odorless, and compare it with the smoke-enveloped flame on the Altar of Burnt Offerings, which in a certain sense generated darkness rather than dispelled it. But there is a still deeper and more sublime meaning in this fire symbol, which we will not take up for discussion until we come to the SHEKINAH GLORY, whose dazzling brilliance hovered over the Mercy Seat in the WEST ROOM. Before we can enter into this subject, we must understand all the symbols that lie between the Golden Candlestick and that sublime Father Fire which was the crowning glory of the Holy of Holies, the most sacred part of the Tabernacle in the Wilderness.

THE TABLE OF SHEWBREAD

The East Room of the Temple may be called the Hall of Service, for it corresponds to the three years' ministry of Christ, and contains all the paraphernalia for soul growth, though, as said, furnished with only three principal articles. Among the chief of these is the Table of Shewbread. Upon this table, as we have already seen, there were two piles of shewbread, each containing six loaves, and upon the top of each pile there was a little heap of frankincense. The aspirant who came to the Temple door "poor, naked, and blind" has since been brought to the light of the Seven-branched Candlestick, obtaining a certain amount of cosmic knowledge, and THIS HE IS REQUIRED TO USE IN THE SERVICE OF HIS FELLOW MEN; the Table of Shewbread represents this in symbol.

The grain from which this shewbread was made had been originally given by God, but then it was planted by mankind, who had previously plowed and tilled the soil. After planting their grain they must cultivate and water it; then when the grain had borne fruit according to the nature of the soil and the care bestowed upon it, it had to be harvested, threshed, ground, and baked. Then the ancient SERVANTS OF GOD had to carry it into the Temple, where it was placed before the Lord as bread to "SHEW" THAT THEY HAD PERFORMED THEIR TOIL AND RENDERED THE NECESSARY SERVICE.

The God-given grains of wheat in the twelve loaves represent the OPPORTUNITIES FOR SOUL GROWTH given by God, which come to all through the twelve departments of life represented by the twelve houses of the horoscope, under the dominion of the twelve divine Hierarchies known through the signs of the zodiac. BUT IT IS THE TASK OF THE MYSTIC MASON, THE TRUE TEMPLE BUILDER, TO EMBRACE THESE OPPORTUNITIES, TO CULTIVATE AND NOURISH THEM SO THAT HE MAY

REAP THEREFROM THE LIVING BREAD WHICH NUR-
TURES THE SOUL.

We do not, however, assimilate our physical food IN TOTO;
there is a residue, a large proportion of ash, left after we have
amalgamated the quintessence into our system. Similarly, the
shewbread was not burned or consumed before the Lord, but two
small heaps of frankincense were placed on the two stacks of
shewbread, one on each pile. This was conceived to be the aroma
thereof, and was later burned on the Altar of Incense. Likewise the
soul sustenance of service gathered daily by the ardent Mystic Mason is thrown into the mill of retrospection at eventide when he
retires to his couch and performs there the scientific exercises
given by the Elder Brothers of the Rose Cross.

There is a time each month which is particularly propitious for
extracting the frankincense of soul growth and burning it before
the lord so that it may be a sweet savor, TO BE AMALGA-
MATED WITH THE SOUL BODY and form part of that golden,
radiant "wedding garment." This as at the time when the moon is at
the full. Then she is in the east, and the heavens are ablaze with
light as was the East Room of the ancient Atlantean Mystery Temple where the priest garnered the pabulum of the soul, symbolized
by the shewbread and the fragrant essence, which delighted our
Father in Heaven then as now.

Let the Mystic Mason take particular note, however, that the
loaves of shewbread were not the musings of dreamers; they were
not the product of speculation upon the nature of God or light.
THEY WERE THE PRODUCT OF ACTUAL TOIL, of orderly
systematic work, and it behooves us to follow the path of actual
service if we would garner treasure in heaven. Unless we really
WORK and SERVE humanity, we shall have nothing to bring, no
bread to "shew," at the Feast of the Full Moon; and at the mystic
marriage of the higher to the lower self we shall find ourselves mi-
nus the radiant golden sold body, the mystic wedding garment

without which the union with Christ can never be consummated.

THE ALTER OF INCENSE

At the Altar of Incense, as we saw in the general description of the Tabernacle and its furniture, incense was offered before the lord continually, and the priest who stood before the altar ministering was at that time looking toward the mercy Seat over the Ark, though it as impossible for him to see it because of the SECOND VEIL which was interposed between the first and second apartments of the Tabernacle, the Holy Place and the Holy of Holies. We have also seen in the consideration of the "shewbread" that INCENSE symbolizes the extract, THE AROMA OF THE SERVICE we have rendered according to our opportunities; and just as the sacrificial animal upon the Brazen Altar represents the deeds of wrongdoing committed during the day, so the incense burned upon the Golden Altar, which is a sweet savor to the Lord, represents the virtuous deeds of our lives.

CHAPTER FOUR

THE ARK OF THE COVENANT

It is noteworthy and fraught with great mystic significance that the aroma of VOLUNTARY SERVICE is represented as SWEET-SMELLING, FRAGRANT INCENSE, while the odor of sin, selfishness, and transgression of the law, represented by COMPULSORY SACRIFICE upon the Altar of service, is nauseating; for it needs no great imagination to understand that the cloud of smoke which went up continually from the burning carcasses of the sacrificial animals created a nauseating stench to show the exceeding loathsomeness of it, while the perpetual incense offered upon the Altar before the second veil showed by antithesis the beauty and sublimity of selfless service, thus exhorting the Mystic Mason, as a CHILD OF LIGHT, to shun the one and cleave to the other.

Let it be understood also that SERVICE does not consist in doing great things only. Some of the heroes, so-called were mean and small in their general lives, and rose only to the occasion upon one great and notable day. Martyrs have been put on the calendar of saints because they DIED for a cause; but it is a greater heroism, it is a greater martyrdom sometimes, to do the little things that no one notices and sacrifice self IN SIMPLE SERVICE TO OTHERS.

We have seen previously that the veil at the entrance to the outer court and the veil in front of the East Room of the Tabernacle were both made in four colors, blue, red, purple, and white. But THE SECOND VEIL, which divided the East Room of the Tabernacle from the West Room, differed with respect to make-up from the other two. It was wrought with the figures of Cherubim. We will not consider, however, the significance of this fact until we take up the subject of the NEW MOON AND INITIATION, but will now look into the second apartment of the Tabernacle, the western room, called the Most Holy or the Holy of Holies. Beyond the second veil, into this second apartment, no mortal might ever pass save the HIGH PRIEST, and he was only allowed to enter on one occasion in the whole year, namely, Yom Kippur, the Day of Atonement, and then only after the most solemn preparation and with the most reverential care. The Holiest of All was clothed with the solemnity of another world; it was filled with an unearthly grandeur. The whole Tabernacle was the sanctuary of God, but here in this place was the awful abode of His presence, the special dwelling place of the SHEKINAH GLORY, and well might mortal man tremble to present himself within these sacred precincts, as the High Priest must do on the Day of Atonement.

In the westernmost end of this apartment, the western end of the whole Tabernacle, rested the "ARK OF THE COVENANT." It was a hollow receptacle containing the GOLDEN POT OF MANNA, AARON'S ROD THAT BUDDED, AND THE TABLES OF THE LAW which were given to Moses. While this Ark of the Covenant remained in the Tabernacle in the Wilderness, TWO STAVES WERE ALWAYS WITHIN THE FOUR RINGS OF THE ARK so that it could be picked up instantly and moved, but when the Ark as finally taken to Solomon's Temple, the staves were taken out. This is very important in its symbolical significance. Above the Ark hovered the Cherubim, and between them dwelt the uncreated glory of God. "Three," said He to Moses, "I will meet with thee, and I will commune with thee from above the Mercy Seat, from between the two Cherubim which are upon the Ark of the Testimony."

The glory of the Lord seen above the Mercy Seat was in the appearance of a cloud. The Lord said to Moses, "Speak unto Aaron they brother that he come not at all time into the Holiest Place within the veil before the Mercy Seat which is upon the Ark, that he die not, for I will appear in the cloud upon the Mercy Seat." This manifestation of the divine presence was called among the Jews the SHEKINAH GLORY. Its appearance was attended no doubt with a wonderful spiritual glory of which it is impossible to

24

form any proper conception. Out of this cloud the voice of God was heard with deep solemnity when He was consulted in behalf of the people.

When the aspirant has qualified to enter into this place behind the second veil, he finds everything DARK to the physical eye, and it is necessary that he should have another light WITHIN. When he first came to the eastern Temple gate, he was "POOR, NAKED, AND BLIND," asking for LIGHT. He was then shown the dim light which appeared in the smoke above the Altar of sacrifice, and told that in order to advance he must kindle within himself that flame by remorse for wrongdoing. Later on he was shown the more excellent light in the East Room of the Tabernacle, which proceeded from the Seven- branched Candlestick; in other words he was given the light of knowledge and of reason that by it he might advance further upon the path. But it was required that BY SERVICE he should evolve within himself and around himself another light, the golden "wedding garment," which is also THE CHRIST LIGHT OF THE SOUL BODY. By lives of service this glorious soul- substance gradually pervades his whole aura until it is ablaze with a golden light. Not until he has evolved this INNER illumination can he enter into the darkened precincts of the second Tabernacle, as the Most Holy place is sometimes called.

"GOD IS LIGHT; if we walk in the light as He is in the Light, we have fellowship one with another." This is generally taken to indicate only the fellowship of the Saints, but as a matter of fact it applies also to the fellowship which we have with God. When the disciple enters the second Tabernacle, THE LIGHT WITHIN HIMSELF VIBRATES TO THE LIGHT OF THE SHEKINAH GLORY between the Cherubim, and he realizes the fellowship with his FATHER FIRE.

As the Cherubim and the Father Fire which hover above the Ark represent the divine Hierarchies which overshadow mankind during his pilgrimage through the wilderness, so THE ARK WHICH IS FOUND THERE REPRESENTS MAN IN HIS HIGHEST

DEVELOPMENT. Three were, as already said, three things within the Ark: the Golden Pot of Manna, the Budding Rod, and the Tables of the Law. When the aspirant stood at the eastern gate as a child of sin, THE LAW WAS WITHOUT AS A TASKMASTER to bring him to Christ. It exacted with unrelenting severity an eye for an eye and a tooth for a tooth. Every transgression brought a just recompense, and man was circumscribed on every hand by laws commanding him to do certain things and refrain from doing others. But when THROUGH SACRIFICE AND SERVICE he has finally arrived at the stage of evolution represented by the Ark in the western room of the Tabernacle, the TABLES OF THE LAW ARE WITHIN. He has then become emancipated from all outside interference with his actions; not that he would break any laws, but because HE WORKS WITH THEM. Just as we have learned to respect the property right of others and have therefore become emancipated from the commandment. "Thou shalt not steal," so he who keeps all laws because he wants to do so has on that account no longer need of an exterior taskmaster, but gladly renders obedience in all things because HE IS A SERVANT OF THE LAW AND WORKS WITH IT, FROM CHOICE AND NOT THROUGH NECESSITY.

THE GOLDEN POT OF MANNA

Manas, mensch, mens, or man is readily associated with the MANNA that came down from heaven. it is the HUMAN SPIRIT that descended from our Father above for a pilgrimage through matter, and the Golden Pot wherein it was kept symbolizes the golden aura of the soul body.

Although the Bible story is not in strict accordance with the events, it gives the main facts of the mystic manna which fell from heaven. When we want to learn what is the nature of this so-called

BREAD, we may turn to the sixth chapter of the Gospel of John, which relates how Christ fed the multitudes with LOAVES AND FISHES, symbolizing the mystic doctrine of the 2000 years which He was then ushering in, for during that time the sun BY PRECESSION OF THE EQUINOX has been passing through the sign of the fishes, Pisces, and the people have been taught to abstain at least one day during the week (Friday) and at a certain time of the year from the fleshpots which belonged to Egypt or ancient Atlantis. They have been given the Piscean water at the temple door, and the Virginian Wafers at the communion table before the altar when they worshiped the Immaculate Virgin, representing the celestial sign Virgo (which is opposite the sign Pisces), and entered communion with the sun begotten by her.

Christ also explained at that time in mystic but unmistakable language what that LIVING BREAD, or manna, was, namely, the Ego. This explanation will be found in verses thirty-three and thirty-five, where we read: "For the bread of God is he which cometh down from heaven and giveth light unto the world--I am (EGO SUM) THE BREAD OF LIFE." This, then, is the symbol of the golden pot of manna which was found in the Ark. This manna is the Ego or human spirit, which gives life to the organisms that we behold in the physical world. It is hidden within the Ark of each human being, and the Golden pot or soul body or "wedding garment" is also latent within every one. It is made more massive, lustrous, and resplendent by the spiritual alchemy whereby service is transmuted to soul growth. It is THE HOUSE NOT MADE WITH HANDS, eternal in the heavens, wherewith Paul longed to be clothed, as said in the Epistle to the Corinthians. Every one who is striving to aid his fellow men thereby garners within himself that golden treasure, laid up in heaven, where neither moth nor rust can destroy it.

AARON'S ROD

An ancient legend relates that when Adam was expelled from the Garden of Eden, he took with him three slips of the TREE OF LIFE, which were then planted by Seth. Seth, the second son of Adam, is, according to the Masonic legend, father of the spiritual hierarchy of CHURCHMEN working with humanity through Catholicism, while the sons of Cain are the CRAFTSMEN of the world. The latter are active in Freemasonry, promoting material and industrial progress, as builders of the temple of Solomon, the universe, should be. The three sprouts planted by Seth have had important missions in the spiritual development of humanity, and one of them is said to be the Rod of Aaron.

In the beginning of concrete existence generation was carried on under the wise guidance of the angels, who saw to it that the creative act was accomplished at times when the interplanetary rays of force were propitious; and man was also forbidden to eat of the Tree of Knowledge. The nature of that tree is readily determined from such sentences as "Adam KNEW his wife, and she bore Cain"; "Adam KNEW his wife, and she bore Seth'; "how shall I bear a child seeing that I KNOW not a man?" as said by Mary to the angel Gabriel. In the light of this interpretation the STATEMENT of the Angel (it was not a curse) when he discovered that his precepts had been disobeyed, namely, "dying thou shalt die," is also intelligible, for the bodies generated regardless of cosmic influences could not be expected to persist. Hence man was exiled from the etheric realms of spiritual force (Eden), where grows the tree of vital power; exiled to concrete existence in the dense physical bodies which he has made for himself by generation. This was surely a blessing, for who has a body sufficiently good and perfect in his own estimation that he would like to live in it forever? Death, then, is a boon to the spiritual realms for a season, and build better vehicles each time we return to earth life. As Oliver Wendell

Holmes says:

"Build thee more stately mansions, O my soul!
As the swift seasons roll.
Leave thy low-vaulted past,
Let each new temple, nobler than the last,
Shut tree from Heaven with a dome more vast,
Till thou at length art free,
Leaving thine outgrown shell
by life's unresting sea."

In the course of time when we learn to shun the pride of life and the lust of the flesh, generation will cease to sap our vitality. The vital energy will then be used for regeneration, and the spiritual powers, symbolized by Aaron's Rod, will be developed.

The wand of the magician, the holy spear of Parsifal the Grail king, and the budding Rod of Aaron are emblems of this divine creative force, which works wonders of such a nature that we call them miracles. But let it be clearly understood that no one who has evolved to the point in evolution where he is symbolized by the Ark of the Covenant in the West Room of the Tabernacle ever uses this power for selfish ends. When Parsifal, the hero of the soul myth by that name, had witnessed the temptation of Kundry and proved himself to be emancipated from the greatest sin of all, the sin of lust and unchastity, he recovered the sacred spear taken by the black magician, Klingsor, from the fallen and unchaste rail king, Amfortas. Then for many years he traveled in the world, seeking again the Castle of the Grail, and he said: "Often was I sorely beset by enemies and tempted to use the spear in self-defense, but I knew that THE SACRED SPEAR MUST NEVER BE USED TO HURT, ONLY TO HEAL."

An that is the attitude of everyone who develops within him the budding Rod of Aaron. Though he may turn this spiritual faculty to good account in order to provide bread for a multitude, he would never think of turning a single stone to bread FOR HIMSELF that his hunger might be appeased. Though he were nailed to the cross to die, he would not free himself by spiritual power which he had readily exercised to save others from the grave. Though he were reviled every day of his life as a fraud or charlatan, he would never misuse his spiritual power to show a sign whereby the world might know without the shadow of a doubt that he was regenerate or heaven-born. This was the attitude of Christ Jesus, and its has been and is imitated by everyone who is a Christ-in-the-making.

CHAPTER FIVE

THE SACRED SHEKINAH GLORY

The Western Room of the Tabernacle was as dark as the heavens are at the time when the lesser light, the moon, is in the western portion of sky at eventide with the sun; that is to say, at the new moon, which begins a new cycle in a new sign of the zodiac. In the westernmost part of this darkened sanctuary stood the Ark of the Covenant, with the Cherubim hovering above, and also the fiery Shekinah Glory, out of which the Father of Light communed with His worshipers, but which to the physical vision was invisible and therefore dark.

We do not usually realize that the whole world is afire, that fire is in the water, that it burns continually in plant, animal, and man; yes, there is nothing in the work that is not ensouled by fire. The reason why we do not perceive this more clearly is that we cannot dissociate fire and flame. But as a matter of fact, FIRE bears the same relation to FLAME as SPIRIT to the BODY; it is the unseen but potent power of manifestation. In other words, the true fire is dark, invisible to the physical sight. IT IS ONLY CLOTHED IN FLAME WHEN CONSUMING PHYSICAL MATTER. Consider, for illustration, how fire leaps out of the flint when struck, and how a gas flame has the darkened core beneath the light-giving portion; also how a wire may carry electricity and be perfectly cold, yet it will emit a flame under certain conditions.

At this point it may be expedient to mark the difference between the Tabernacle in the Wilderness, Solomon's Temple, and the later Temple built by Herod. There is a very vital difference. Both the MIRACULOUSLY ENKINDLED FIRE on the Brazen Altar in the eastern part of the Tabernacle and the invisible SHEKINAH GLORY in the distant western part of the sanctuary were also present in Solomon's Temple. These were thus sanctuaries in a sense not equaled by the Temple built by Herod. The latter was, nevertheless, in a sense the most glorious of the three, for IT WAS GRACED BY THE BODILY PRESENCE OF OUR LORD, CHRIST JESUS, IN WHOM DWELT THE GODHEAD. Christ made the first self-sacrifice, thereby abrogating the sacrifice of animals, and finally at the consummation of His work in the visible world RENT THE VEIL and opened a way into the Holy of Holies, not only for the favored few, the priests and Levites, but that WHOSOEVER WILL may come and serve the Deity whom we know as our Father. Having fulfilled the law and the prophets Christ has done away with the OUTWARD sanctuary, and from henceforth the Altar of Burnt Offerings must be set up WITHIN the heart to atone for wrongdoing; the Golden Candlestick must be lighted WITHIN the heart to guide us upon our way, as the Christ WITHIN, the Shekinah Glory of the Father, must dwell WITHIN the sacred precincts of our own God Consciousness.

THE SHADOW OF THE CROSS

Paul in his letter to the Hebrews gives a description of the Tabernacle and much information about the customs used there which it would benefit the student to know. Among other things note that he calls the Tabernacle "a shadow of good things to come." There is in this ancient Mystery Temple a promise given which has not yet been fulfilled, a promise that holds good today just as well as upon the day it was given. If we visualize in our mind the arrangement of things inside the Tabernacle, we shall readily see the shadow of the Cross. Commencing at the eastern gate there was the ALTAR OF BURNT OFFERINGS; a little farther along the path to the Tabernacle itself we find the LAVER OF CONSECRATION, the Molten Sea, in which the priests washed. Then upon entering the East Room of the Temple we find an article of furniture, THE GOLDEN CANDLESTICK, at the EXTREME LEFT, and the TABLE OF SHEWBREAD at the EXTREME RIGHT, the two forming a cross with the path we have been pursuing toward and within the Tabernacle. In the center in front of the second veil we find the ALTAR OF INCENSE, which forms the center of the cross, while the Ark placed in the westernmost part of the West Room, the Holy of Holies, gives the short or upper limb of the cross. In this manner the symbol of spiritual unfoldment which is our particular ideal today was shadowed forth in the ancient Mystery Temple, and that consummation which is attained at the end of the cross, the achievement of getting the law WITHIN as it was within the Ark itself, is the one that we must all concern ourselves with at the present time. The light that shines over the Mercy Seat in the Holy of Holies at the head of the cross, at the end of the path in this world, is a light or reflection from the invisible world into which the candidate seeks to enter when all the world has grown dark and black about him. Only when we have attained to that stage where we perceive the spiritual light that beckons us on, the light that floats over the Ark, only when we stand in the shadow of the cross, can we really know the meaning, the object, and the goal of life.

At present we may take the opportunities which are offered and perform service more or less efficiently, but it is only when we have by that service evolved the spiritual light WITHIN ourselves, which is the SOUL BODY, and when we have thus gained admission to the West Room, called the Hall of Liberation, that we can really perceive and understand why we are in the world, and what we need in order to make ourselves properly useful. We may not remain, however, when access has been gained. The High Priest was only allowed to enter ONCE A YEAR; there was a very long interval of time between these glimpses of the real purpose of existence. In the times between it was necessary for the High Priest to go out and function among his brethren, humanity, and serve them to the very best of his ability, also to sin, because he was not yet perfect, and then reenter the Holy of Holies after having made proper amends for his sins.

Similar it is with ourselves at this day. We at times attain glimpses of the things that are in store for us and the things we must do to follow Christ to that place where He went. You remember that He said to His disciples: Ye cannot follow me now, but ye shall follow me later. And so it is with us. We have to look again and again into the darkened temple, the Holy of Holies, before we are really fit to stay there; before we are really fitted to take the last step and leap to the summit of the cross, THE PLACE OF THE SKULL, that point in our heads where the spirit takes its departure when it finally leaves the body, or off and on as an Invisible Helper. That Golgotha is the ultimate of human attainment, and we must be prepared to enter the darkened room many times before we are fitted for the final climax.

THE FULL MOON AS A FACTOR IN SOUL GROWTH

Let us now consider the Path of Initiation as symbolically shown in the ancient Temples with the Ark, Fire, and Shekinah, and in the later Temples where Christ taught. Note first that when man was expelled from the Garden of Eden because he had eaten of the Tree of Knowledge, Cherubim guarded the entrance with a flaming sword. Passages like the following, "Adam KNEW Eve, and she bore Abel"; "Adam KNEW Eve, and she bore Seth"; "Elkanah KNEW Hannah, and she bore Samuel"; also Mary's question to the angel Gabriel, "How shall I conceive seeing that I KNOW not a man?" all show plainly that indulgence of the passions in the creative act was meant by the phrase, "eating the Tree of Knowledge." When the creative act was performed under inauspicious planetary rays it was a sin committed against the laws of nature, which brought pain and death into the world, estranged us from our primal guardians, and forced us to roam the wilderness of the world for ages.

At the gate of the mystic Temple of Solomon we find the Cherubim, but the fiery sword is not longer in their hand; instead they hold a FLOWER, a symbol full of mystic meaning. Let us compare man with a flower that we may know the great import and significance of this emblem. Man takes his good by way of the head, whence it goes downward. The plant takes nourishment through the root and forces it upward. Man is passionate in love, and he turns the generative organ toward the earth and hides it in shame because of this taint of passion. The plant knows no passion, fertilization is accomplished in the most pure and chaste manner imaginable, therefore it projects its generative organ, the flower, TOWARD THE SUN, a thing of beauty which delights all who behold it. Passionate fallen man exhales THE DEADLY CARBON DIOXIDE; the chaste flower inhales this poison, transmutes it, and gives it back pure, sweet, and scented, a fragrant elixir of life.

This was the mystery of the Grail Cup; this is the emblematic significance of the Cup of Communion, which is called "KELCH" in German "Calix" in Latin, both names signifying the seed pod of the flower. The Communion Cup with its mystic blood cleansed from the passion incident to generation brings to him who truly drinks thereof eternal life, and thus it becomes the vehicle of regeneration, of the mystic birth into a higher sphere, a "foreign country," where he who has served his apprenticeship in Temple building and has mastered the "art and crafts" of this world may learn higher things.

The symbol of the Cherubim with the open flower placed upon the door of Solomon's Temple delivers the message to the aspirant that PURITY IS THE KEY by which alone he can hope to unlock the gate to God; or as Christ expressed it, "Blessed are the pure in heart for they shall see God." The flesh must be consumed on the Altar of self-sacrifice, and the sold must be washed in the Laver of Consecration to the higher life where it may approach the Temple door. When "naked," "poor," and "blinded" by tears of contrition it gropes in darkness, seeking the Temple door, it shall find entrance to the Hall of Service, the East Room of the Tabernacle, which is ablaze with light from the Seven-branched Candlestick, emblematic of the luminosity of the full moon, the moon changing in cycles of seven days. In this Hall of Service the aspirant is taught to weave the luminous vesture of flame which Paul called "some psuchicon," or soul body (1st Cor., 15:44), from the aroma of the shewbread.

When we speak of the soul body we mean exactly what we say, and this vehicle is in nowise to be confused with the soul that permeates it. The Invisible Helper who uses it on soul flights knows it to be as real and tangible as the dense body of flesh blood. But within that golden "wedding garment" there is an INTANGIBLE SOMETHING cognized by the spirit of introspection. It is unnamable and indescribable; it evades the most persistent efforts to fathom it, yet it is there just as certainly as the vehicle which it fills-yes, and more so. It is not life, love, beauty, wisdom, nor can any other human concept convey an idea of what it is, for it is the sum of all human faculties, attributes, and concepts of good, immeasurably intensified. If everything else were taken from us, that prime reality would still remain, and we should be rich in its possession, for through it we feel the drawing power of our Father in Heaven, that inner urge which all aspirants know so well.

To this inner something Christ referred when He said: No man cometh to me except my Father draw him. Just as the true fire is hidden in the flame that encloses it, so that unnamable, intangible something hides in the soul body and burns up the frankincense extracted from the shewbread; thus it lights the fire which makes the soul body luminous. And the AROMA OF LOVING SERVICE to others penetrates the veil as a sweet savor to God, who dwells in the Shekinah Glory similar created above the Ark in the innermost sanctuary, the Holy of Holies.

CHAPTER SIX

THE NEW MOON AND INITIATION

When the candidate entered at the eastern gate of the Temple looking for light, he was confronted by the fire on he Altar of Burnt Offerings, which emitted a dim light enveloped in clouds of smoke. He was then in the spiritually darkened condition of the ordinary man; he lacked the light within and therefore it was necessary to give him the light without. But when he has arrived at the point when he is ready to have evolved the luminous soul body in the service of humanity. Then he is thought to have the light within himself, "the light that lighteth every man." Unless he has that, he cannot enter the dark room of the Temple.

What takes place secretly in the Temple is shown openly in the heavens. As the moon gathers light from the sun during her passage from the new to the full, so the man who treads the path of holiness by use of his golden opportunities in the East Room of selfless service gathers the materials wherewith to make his luminous "wedding garment," and that material is best amalgamated on the night of the full moon. But conversely, as the moon gradually dissipates the accumulated light and draws nearer the sun in order to make a fresh start upon a new cycle at the time of the new moon, so also according to the law of analogy those who have gathered their treasures and laid them up in heaven by service are at a certain time of the month closer to their Source and their Maker, their Father Fire in the higher spheres, than at any other time. As the great saviors of mankind are born at the winter solstice on the longest and darkest night of the year, so also the process of Initiation which brings to birth in the invisible world one of the lesser saviors, THE INVISIBLE HELPER, is most easily accomplished on the longest and darkest night of the month, that is to say, on the night of the new moon when the lunar orb is in the westernmost part of the heavens.

All occult development begins with the vital body, and the keynote of that vehicle is "repetition." To get the best out of any subject repetition is necessary. In order to understand the final consummation to which all this has been leading up, let us take a final look from another angle at the three kinds of fire within the Temple.

Near the eastern gate was the Altar of Burnt Offering. On that altar smoke was continually generated by the bodies of the sacrifices, and the pillar of smoke was seen far and wide by the multitude who were instructed in the inner mysteries of life. The flame, the light, hidden in this cloud of smoke was at best but dimly perceived. This showed that the great majority of mankind are taught principally by the immutable laws of nature, which exact from them a sacrifice whether they know it or not. As the flame of purification was then fed by the more coarsely constructed and baser bodies of animal sacrifices, exacted under the Mosaic law, so also today the baser and more passionate mass of humanity is being brought into subjection by fear of punishment by the law in the present world-more than by apprehension of what my follow in the world to come.

A light of a different nature shone in the East Room of the Tabernacle. Instead of drawing its nourishment from the sinful and passionate flesh of the animal sacrifices, it was fed by olive oil procured from the chaste plant kingdom; and its flame was not shrouded in smoke, but was clear and distinct, so that it might illuminate the room and guide the priests, who were the servants of the Temple, in their ministrations. The priests were endeavoring to work in harmony with the divine plan, therefore they saw the light more clearly that the uninstructed and careless multitude. Today also the mystic light shines for all who are endeavoring to really serve at the shrine of self-sacrifice-particularly for the pledged pupils of a Mystery School such as the Rosicrucian Order. They are waling in a light not seen by the multitude, and if they are really serving, they have the true guidance of the Elder Brothers of humanity, who are always ready to help them at the difficult points on the Path.

But the most sacred fire of all was the Shekinah Glory in the West Room of the Tabernacle above the Mercy Seat. As this West Room was dark, we understand that it was an invisible fire, a light from another world.

Now mark this, the fire that was shrouded in smoke and flame upon the Altar of Burnt Offerings, consuming the sacrifices brought there in expiation of sins committed under the law, was the symbol of JEHOVAH THE LAWGIVER; and we remember that the law was given to brings us to Christ. The clear and beautiful light which shone in the Hall of Service, the East Room of the Tabernacle, is the golden-hued Christ light, which guides those who endeavor to follow in His steps upon the path of self-forgetting service.

As the Christ said, "I go to my Father," when He was about to be crucified, so also the Servant of the Cross who has made the most of his opportunities in the visible world is allowed to enter the glory of his Father Fire, the invisible Shekinah Glory. He ceases then to see through the dark glass of the body, and beholds his Father face to face in the invisible realms of nature.

The church steeple is very broad at the bottom, but gradually it narrows more and more until at the top it is just a point with the cross above it. So it is with the path of holiness; at the beginning there are many things which we may permit ourselves, but as we advance, one after another of these digressions must be done away with, and we must devote ourselves more and more exclusively to the service of holiness. At last there comes a point where this path is as sharp as the razor's edge, and we can then only grasp at the cross. But when we have attained that point, when we can climb this narrowest of all paths, then we are fitted to follow Christ into the beyond and serve there as we have served here.

Thus this ancient symbol shadowed forth the trial and triumph of the faithful servant, and thought it has been superseded by other and greater symbols holding forth a higher ideal and a greater promise, the basic principles embodies in it are as valid today as ever.

In the Altar of Burnt Offerings we see clearly the nauseating nature of sin and the necessity of expiation and justification.

By the Molten Sea we are still taught that we must live the stainless life that of holiness and consecration.

From the East Room we learn today how to make diligent use of our opportunities to grow the golden grain of selfless service and make that "living bread" which feeds the soul, the Christ within.

And when we have ascended the steps of Justification, Consecration, and Self-Abnegation, we reach the West Room, which is the threshold of Liberation. Over it we are conducted into greater realms, where greater soul unfoldment may be accomplished.

But through this ancient Temple stands no longer upon the plains where the wandering hosts pitched their camps in the hoary past, it may be made a much more potent factor for soul growth by any aspirant of today that it was by the ancient Israelites provided he will build it according to pattern. Nor need the lack of gold wherewith to build distress anyone, for now the true tabernacle must be built in heaven-and "HEAVEN IS WITH YOU." To build well and true, according to the rules of the ancient craft of Mystic Masonry, the aspirant must learn first to build within himself the altar with its sacrifices, then he must watch and pray while patiently waiting for the divine fire to consume offering. Then he must bathe himself with tears of contrition till he has washed away the stains of sin. Meanwhile he must keep the lamp of divine guidance filled that he may perceive how, when, and where to serve; he must work hard to have abundance of "bread of shew," and the incense of aspiration and prayer must be ever in his heart and on his lips. Then YOM KIPPUR, the Great Day of At-one-ment, will surely find him ready to go to his Father, and learn how better to help his younger brothers to ascent the Path.

PART II

THE CHRISTIAN MYSTIC INITIATION

CHAPTER ONE

THE ANNUNCIATION AND IMMACULATE CONCEPTION

Much is said in certain classes of the Western World about Initiation. This in the minds of most people seems usually to be associated with the occultism taught in the religions of the far East; something that is peculiar to the devotees of Buddhism, Hinduism, and kindred systems of faith, and which in nowise appertains to the religion of the Western World, particularly to the Christian religion.

We have shown in the preceding series on "Symbols and Ancient and Modern Initiation: that this idea is entirely gratuitous, and that the ancient Tabernacle in the Wilderness pictures in its symbolism the path of progression from childlike ignorance to superhuman knowledge. As the VEDAS brought light to the devotees who worshiped in faith and fervor on the banks of the Ganges in the sunny South, so the Eddas were a guiding star to the sons of the rugged Northland, who sought the Light of life in ancient Iceland where the sturdy Vikings steered their ships in frozen seas. "Arjuna," who fights the noble fight in the "Mahabharata," or "Great War," constantly being waged between the higher and the lower self, difference in nowise from the hero of the northern soul myth, "Siegfried," which means, "He who through victory gains peace."

Both are representative of the candidate undergoing Initiation. And though their experiences in this great adventure vary in certain respects called for by the temperamental differences of the northern and southern peoples, and provided for in the respective schools to which they are referred for soul growth, the main features are identical, and the end, which is enlightenment, is the same. Aspiring souls have walked to the Light in the brilliantly illuminated Persian temples where the sun god in his blazing chariot

44

was the symbol of Light, as well as under the mystic magnificence of the iridescence shed abroad by the aurora borealis of the frozen North. That the true Light of the deepest esoteric knowledge has always been present in all ages, even the darkest of the so-called dark, there is ample evidence to show.

Raphael used his wonderful skill with the brush to embody it in two of his great paintings, "The Sistine Madonna" and the "Marriage of the Virgin," which we would advise the interested reader to examine for himself. Copies of these paintings are procurable in almost any art store. In the original there is a peculiar tint of golden haze behind the Madonna and Child, which though exceedingly crude to one gifted with spiritual sight, is nevertheless as close an imitation of the basic color of the first-heaven world as it is possible to make with the pigments of earth. Close inspection of this background will reveal the fact that it is composed of a multitude of what we are used to call "angel" heads and wings.

This again is as literal a pictorial representation of facts concerning the inhabitants of that world as could be given, for during the process of purgation which takes place in the lower regions of the Desire World the lower parts of the body are actually disintegrated so that only the head, containing the intelligence of the man, remains when he enters the first heaven, a fact which has puzzled many who have happened to see the souls there. The wings of course have no reality outside the picture, but were placed there to show ability to move swiftly, which is inherent in all beings in the invisible worlds. The People is represented as pointing to the Madonna and the Christ Child, and a close examination of the hand wherewith he points will show that it has six fingers. There is not historical evidence to show that the Pontiff actually had such a deformity, neither can that fact be an accident; the six fingers in the painting must therefore have been due to design on the part of the painter.

What its purpose was we shall learn by examination of the "Marriage of the Virgin," where a similar anomaly may be noted. In that picture Mary and Joseph are represented together with he Christ Child under such conditions that it is evident that they are just on the eve of departure for Egypt, and a Rabbi is in the act of joining them in wedlock. The left foot of Joseph is the foremost object in the picture, and if we count we shall find it represented as having six toes. By the six fingers in the Pope's picture and the six toes of Joseph, Raphael wants to show us that both possessed a sixth sense such as is awakened by Initiation. By this subtle sense the foot of Joseph was guided in its flight to keep secure that sacred things which had been entrusted to his care. To the other was given a sixth sense that he might not be a blind leader of the blind but might have the "seeing eye" required to point out the Way, the Truth, and the Life. And it is a fact, though not commonly known, that with one or two exceptions when political power was strong enough to corrupt the College of Cardinals, all who have sat upon the so-called throne of Peter have had the spiritual sight in a greater or lesser degree.

We have seen in the articles on "Symbols of Ancient and Modern Initiation," which preceded the present article, that the Atlantean Mystery Temple known as the Tabernacle in the Wilderness was a school of soul growth; and it should not surprise us to learn that the four Gospels containing the life of Christ are also formulae of Initiation, revealing another and a later Path to power. In the ancient Egyptian Mysteries, Horus was the first fruit whom the aspirant endeavored to imitate, and it is significant that in the Ritual of Initiation which was in vogue in that day and which we now call the "Book of the Dead," the aspirant to Initiation was always addressed Horus so-and-so. Following the same method today we might appropriately address those following the Christian Path of Initiation as Christ so-and-so, for as a matter of fact all who tread this Path are really Christs-in-the-making. Each in his or her turn will reach the different stations of the Via Dolorosa, or Path of Sorrow, which leads to Calvary, and experience in his or her own body the pangs and pains suffered by the Hero of the Gospels. Initiation is a cosmic process of enlightenment and evolution of power; therefore the experiences of all are similar in the main features.

The Christian Mystic form of Initiation differs radically from the Rosicrucian method, which aims to bring the candidate to compassion through knowledge, and therefore seeks to cultivate in him the latent faculties of spiritual sight and hearing at the very start of his career as an aspirant to the higher life. it teaches him to know the hidden mysteries of being and to perceive intellectually the unity of each with all, so that at last through this knowledge there is awakened within him the feeling that makes him truly realize his oneness with all that lives and moves, which puts him in full and perfect tune with the Infinite, making him a true helper and worker in the divine kingdom of evolution.

The goal attained through the Christian Mystic Initiation is the same, but the method, as said, is entirely different. In the first place, the candidate is usually unconscious of trying to attain any definite object, at least during the first stages of his endeavors, and there is in this noble School of Initiation but no Teacher, the Christ, who is ever before the spiritual vision of the candidate as the Ideal and the Goal of all his striving. The Western world, alas! has become so enmeshed in intellectuality that its aspirants can only enter the Path when their reason has been satisfied; and unfortunately it is a desire for more knowledge which brings most of the pupils to the Rosicrucian School. It is an arduous task to cultivate in them the compassion which must blend with their knowledge and be the guiding factor in the use of it before they are fitted to enter the Kingdom of Christ. But those who are drawn to the Christian Mystic Path feel no difficulty of that nature. They have within themselves an all-embracing love, which urges them onward and eventually generates in them a knowledge which the writer believes to be far superior to that attained by any other method. One who follows the intellectual Path of development is apt to sneer superciliously at another whose temperament impels him along the Mystic Path. Such an attitude of mind is not only detrimental to the spiritual development of whoever entertains it, but it is entirely gratuitous, as the works of Jacob Boehme, Thomas a Kempis, and many other who have followed the Mystic Path will show. The more knowledge we possess the greater condemnation also shall we merit if we do not use it right. But love, which is the basic principle in the Christian Mystic's life, can never bring us into condemnation or conflict with the purposes of God. It is infinitely better to be able to FEEL any noble emotion that to have the keenest intellect and one which is able to define all emotions. Hairsplitting over the constitution and evolution of the atom surely will not promote soul growth as much as humble helpfulness toward our neighbor.

There are nine definite steps in the Christian Mystic Initiation, commencing with the Baptism, which is dedicatory. The Annunciation and Immaculate Conception precede as matters of course for reasons given later. Having prepared our minds by the foregoing consideration, we are now ready to consider each stage separately in this glorious process of spiritual unfoldment.

THE ANNUNCIATION AND IMMACULATE CONCEPTION

The Christian Mystic is emphatically not the product of one life, but the flower of many preparatory existences, during which he has cultivated that sublime compassion which makes him feel the whole world's woe, and conjures up before his spiritual vision the Christ Ideal as the true balm of Gilead, its practice the only palladium against all human grief and sorrow. Such a soul is watched over special care by the divine Hierarchies who have charge of our progression along the path of evolution, and when the time is ripe for him to enter that life in which he is to run the final race to reach the goal and become a Savior of his kind, angels are indeed watching, waiting, and singing hosannas in joyful anticipation of the great event.

Like always seeks like, and naturally the parents are carefully selected for (and by such a noble soul from among the "sons and daughters of the King." They may be in the poorest circumstances from a worldly point of view; it may be necessary to cradle the babe in a manger, but no richer gift ever came to parents that such a noble soul. Among the qualifications necessary to be the parents of such an Ego is that the mother be a "virgin" and the father a "builder."

It is stated in the Bible that Joseph was a CARPENTER, but the Greek word is "tekton" which means "builder." In Mystic Masonry God is called the Grant Architect. ARCHE is the Greek word signifying primordial substance, and a tekton is a builder. Thus God is the Great Master Builder, who out of primordial substance fashioned the world as an evolutionary field for various grades of beings. He uses in His universe many tektons, or builders, of various grades. Everyone who follows the Path of spiritual attainment, endeavoring to work constructively with the laws of nature as a servant of humanity, is a TEKTON or builder in the sense that he has the qualifications necessary to aid in giving birth to a great soul. Thus when it is said that Jesus was a carpenter and the son of a carpenter, we understand that they were both TEKTONS or builders along cosmic lines.

The Immaculate Conception, like all other sublime mysteries, has been dragged down into the gutter of materiality, and being so sublimely spiritual it has perhaps suffered more by this rude treatment than any other of the spiritual teachings. Perhaps it has suffered even more from the clumsy explanation of ignorant supporters that from the jeers and sneers of the cynic. The doctrine of the Immaculate Conception, as popularly understood, is that about two thousand years ago God in a miraculous manner fertilized a certain Mary who was a virgin, as the result she gave birth to Jesus, an individual who is consequence was the Son of God in a sense different from all other men. There is also in the popular mind the idea that this incident is unique in the history of the world.

It is particularly the latter fallacy which has served to distort the beautiful spiritual truth concerning the Immaculate Conception. It is not unique in any sense. Every great soul who has been born into the world to live a life of sublime saintliness, such as required for the Christian Mystic Initiation, has also found entrance through of immaculate virginity who were not besmirched by passion in the performance of the generative act. Men do not gather grapes of thorns. It is an axiomatic truth that like begets like, and before anyone can become a Savior, he must himself be pure and sinless. He, being pure cannot take birth from one who is vile; HE MUST BE BORN OF VIRGIN PARENTS.

But the virginity to which we refer does not comprehend a merely physical condition. There is not inherent virtue in physical virginity, for all possess it at the beginning of life no matter how vile their disposition may be. The virginity of the mother of a Savior is a quality of the soul, which remains unsullied regardless of the physical act of fertilization. When people perform the first creative act without desire for offspring, merely for gratification of their animal lusts and propensities, they lose the only (physical) virginity they ever possessed; but when prospective parents unite in a spirit of prayer, offering their bodies upon the altar of sacrifice in order to provide an incoming soul with the physical body needed at the present time to further spiritual development, their purity of purpose preserves their virginity and draws a noble soul to their hearth and home. Whether a child is conceived in sin or immaculately depends upon its own inherent soul quality, for that will unerringly draw it to parents of a nature like unto its own. To become the son of a virgin predicates a past career of spirituality for the one who is so born.

The "mystic birth" of a "builder" is a cosmic event of great importance, and it is therefore not surprising that it is pictured in the skies from year to year, showing a graphic symbolism in the great world or macrocosm what will eventually take place in man, the little world or microcosm. We are all destined to experience the things that Jesus experienced, including the Immaculate Conception, which is a prerequisite to the life of saints and saviors of varying degrees. By understanding this great cosmic symbol we shall more easily understand its application to the individual human being. The sun is "THE LIGHT OF THE WORLD" in a material sense. When in winter time it reaches the extreme southern declination at the solstice on December 23rd, the people in the northern hemisphere, where all the present religions have had their birth, are plunged into the deepest darkness and bereft of the all-sustaining vital power emanating from the sun, which is them partly dead so far as its influence upon men in concerned. It is therefore necessary that a new light shine in the darkness, that a SUN OF GOOD be born to same humanity from the cold and famine which must inevitably result if the sun were to remain in the southern position which he occupies at the winter solstice.

On the night between the 24th and 25th of December, the sun having commenced to slowly rise toward the earth's equator, the zodiacal sign of Virgo, the immaculate celestial Virgin, is on the eastern horizon in all northern latitudes (in the hours immediately preceding midnight). In the science of astrology it is the sign and degree on the eastern horizon at the time of birth which determine the form or body of the creature then born. Therefore the Sun of Good is said to have been born of Virgo, the sublime celestial Virgin, who remains as pure after giving birth to her Sun Child as she was before. By analogy the Son of God who comes to save his fellow men must also be born of an immaculate spiritual virgin.

From what has been said it is evident that a great period of preparation precedes the entrance of a Christian Mystic into the present sphere of human life, though he in his physical consciousness is usually entirely unaware of the fact of the great adventure in store for him. In all probability his childhood days and early youth will pass in obscurity, while he lives an inner life of unusual depth, unconsciously preparing himself for the Baptism, which is the first of

51

the nine steps of this method of attainment.

CHAPTER TWO

MYSTIC RITE OF BAPTISM

It is noteworthy that nearly all religious systems have prescribed ablutions previous to the performance of religious duties, and the worship performed in the ancient Atlantean Mystery Temple, the Tabernacle in the Wilderness, was no exception, as we have seen from the previous articles on "Symbols of Ancient and Modern Initiation." After having obtained justification by sacrifice on the Brazen Altar, the candidate was compelled to wash in the Laver of Consecration, the Molten Sea, before he was allowed to enter upon the duties of his ministry in the sanctuary proper. And it is in conformity with this rule that we find the Hero of the Gospels going to the river Jordan, where He underwent the mystic rite of Baptism. When He rose, we learn that the Spirit descended upon Him. Therefore it is obvious that those who follow the Christian Mystic Path of Initiation must also be similarly baptized before they can receive the Spirit, which is to be their true guide through all the trials before them.

But what constitutes Baptism is a question which has called forth arguments of almost unbelievable intensity. Some contend that it is a sprinkling with water, and other insist upon the immersion of the whole body. Some say that it is sufficient to take an infant into church, sprinkle it with water despite its protests, and presto! it becomes a Christian, an heir of heaven; whereas should it unfortunately die before this sacred rite is performed, it must inevitably go to hell. Others take the more logical position that the desire of an individual for admission into the church is the prime factor necessary to make the rite effective, and therefore wait until adult age before the performance of the ceremony, which requires an immersion of the whole body in water. But whether the rite is performed in infancy or in later life, it seems strange that momentary immersion or sprinkling with water should have the power to save the soul; and when we examine the subsequent life of those who have thus been baptized, even in adult age and with their full consent and desire, we find little or no improvement in the great majority. Therefore it seems evident that this cannot be the proper rite, because the Spirit has not descended upon them. Consequently we must look for another explanation of what constitutes a true mystic rite of Baptism.

A story is told of an Ottoman king who declared war on a neighboring nation, fought a number of battles against it with varying success, but was finally conquered and taken captive to the palace of the victor, where he was compelled to work in the most menial capacity as a slave. After many years fortune favored him, and he escaped to a far country, where by hard work he acquired a small estate, married, and had a number of children, who grew up around him. Finally he found himself upon his deathbed at a very rip old age, and in the exertion of drawing his last breath he raised himself upon his pillow and looked about him, but there were no sons and daughters there. He was not in the place which he had regarded as home for so many years, but in his own palace which he thought he had left in his youth, and he was as young as when he left it. There he found himself sitting in a chair with a basin of water close to his chin and a servant engaged in washing his hair and beard. He had just immersed his face in the water when the dream of going to war had started, and a lifetime had been lived in dreamland during the few seconds it took until he raised his face. There are thousands of other instances to show that outside the physical world time is nonexistent and the happenings of millennia are easily inspected in a few moments.

It is also well known that when people are under water and in the act of drowning, their whole preceding life is reenacted before their eyes with crystal clarity, even the minutest details which have been forgotten during the passing years standing our sharply. Thus there must be and is a storehouse of events which may be contacted under certain conditions when the senses are stilled and we are near sleep or death.

To make this last sentence clear it should be understood and borne in mind that man is a composite being, having finer vehicles which interpenetrate the physical body, usually regarded as the whole man. During death and sleep this dense body is unconscious on account of a complete separation between it and the finer vehicles; but this separation is only partial during dream-filled sleep and prior to drowning. This condition enables the spirit to impress events upon the brain with more or less accuracy according to circumstances, particularly those incidents which are connected with itself. In the light of these things we shall understand what really constitutes the rite of Baptism.

According to the Nebular Theory that which is now the earth was at one time a luminous fire-mist, which gradually cooled by contact with the cold of space. This meeting of heat with cold generated moisture, which evaporated and rose from the heated center, until the cold condensed it and it fell again as moisture upon the heated world. The surface of the earth being thus subjected to alternate liquidation and evaporation for ages, it finally crystallized into a shell which perfectly covered the fiery center. This soft moisture-laden shell naturally generated a mist, which surrounded the planet as an atmosphere, and this was the cradle of everything that has its being upon the earth: man, animal, and plant.

The Bible describes this condition in the second chapter of Genesis, where we are told that at the time of the first man a mist went up from the earth, "for it had not yet rained." This condition evidently continued until the Flood, when the moisture finally descended and left the atmosphere clear so that the rainbow was seen for the first time, the darkness was dispelled, and the age of alternation, day and night, summer and winter, commenced.

By a study of the cosmology and the pictorial account of evolution given in the Northern Eddas, treasured among the sages of Scandinavia before the Christian Era, we may learn more of this period in the earth's history and the bearing which it has upon our subject. As we teach our children, by means of stories and pictures, truths that hey could not intellectually grasp, so the divine leaders of mankind were wont to teach the infant souls in their charge by pictures and allegories, and through these prepare them for a higher and nobler teaching of a later day. The great epic poem which is called "The Lay of the Niebelung," gives us the story of which we are in search, the cosmic origin of the rite of Baptism and why it is necessarily the preliminary step in the spiritual unfoldment of the Christian Mystic.

The cosmogony of the Eddas is similar to that of the Bible is some respects, and in others gives points which bear out the theory of Laplace. We quote from the poetical version of Oehlenschlaeger:

"In the Being's earliest Dawn
All was one dark abyss,
Nor heaven nor earth was known.
Chill noxious fogs and ice,
North from murk Niflheim's hole,
Piled up in mountains lay;
From Muspel's radiant pole,
Southwards fire held the sway.

"Then after ages passed,
Mid in the chaos met
A warm breath, Niflheim's blast,
Cold with prolific heat.
Hence pregnant drops were formed,
Which by the parent air
From Muspel's region warmed,
Produced great Aurgelmer."

Thus by the action of heat and cold Aurgelmer, or as he is also called, the Giant Ymer, was first formed. This was the pregnant seed ground whence came the spiritual Hierarchies, the spirits of the earth, air, and water, and finally man. At the same time the All-Father created the Cow Audumla, from whose four teats issued four streams of milk, which nourished all beings. These are the four ethers, one of which now sustains mineral, two feed the plant, three the animal, and all four the human kingdom. In the Bible they are the four rivers which went forth out of Eden.

Eventually, as postulated by science, a crust must have been formed by the continued boiling of the water, and from this drying crust a mist must have ascended as taught in the second chapter of Genesis. By degrees the mist must have cooled and condensed, shutting out the light of the sun, so that it would have been impossible for early mankind to perceive the body even had they possessed the physical vision. But under such conditions they had no more need of eyes that a mole which burrows in the ground. They were not blind, however, for we re told that "THEY SAW GOD"; and as "spiritual things (and beings) are spiritually perceived," they must have been gifted with spiritual sight. In the spiritual worlds there is a different standard of reality than here, which is the basis of myths.

Under these conditions there could be no clashing of interests, and humanity regarded itself as the children of one great Father while they lived under the water of ancient Atlantis. Egoism did not come into the world until the mist had condensed and they had left the watery atmosphere of Atlantis. When their eyes had been opened so that they could perceive the physical world and the things therein, when each saw himself or herself as separate and apart from all others, the consciousness of "me and mine, thee and thine," took shape in the nascent minds, and a grasping greed replaced the fellow feeling which obtained under the waters of early Atlantis. From that time to the present stage of egoism has been considered the legitimate attitude, and even in our boasted civilization altruism remains a Utopian dream not to be indulged in by practical people.

Had mankind been allowed to travel the path of egoism without let or hindrance, it is difficult to see where it all would have ended. But under the immutable Law of Consequence every cause must produce an adequate effect; the principle of suffering was born from sin for the benevolent purpose of guiding us back to the path of virtue. It takes much suffering and many lives to accomplish this purpose, but finally when we have become men of sorrows and acquainted with grief, when we have cultivated that keen and ready sympathy which feels all the woe of the world, when the Christ has been born within, there comes to the Christian Mystic that ardent aspiration to seek and to save those who are lost and show them the way to everlasting light and peace.

But to show the way, we must know the way; without a true understanding of the CAUSE OF SORROW we cannot teach others to obtain permanent peace. Nor can this understanding of sorrow, sin, and death be obtained from books, lectures, or even the personal teachings of another; at least an impression sufficiently intense to fill the aspirant's whole being cannot be conveyed in that way. Baptism alone will accomplish the purpose in an adequate manner; therefore the first step in the life of a Christian Mystic is Baptism.

But when we say Baptism, we do not necessarily mean a physical Baptism where the candidate is either sprinkled or immersed and where he makes certain promises to the one who baptizes him. The Mystic Baptism may take place in a desert as easily as on an island, for it is a spiritual process to attain a spiritual purpose. It may take place at any time during the night or day, in summer or winter, for it occurs at the moment when the candidate feels with sufficient intensity the longing to know the cause of sorrow and alleviate it. Then the Spirit is conducted under the waters of Atlantis, where it sees the primal condition of brotherly love and kindness; where it perceives God as the great Father of His children, who are there surrounded by His wonderful love. And by the conscious return to this Ocean of Love, the candidate becomes so thoroughly imbued with the feeling of kinship that the spirit of egoism is banished from him forever. It is because of this saturation with the Universal Spirit that is able later to say: "If a man takes your coat, give him you cloak also; if he asks you to walk one mile with him, go with him two miles." Feeling himself one and all, the candidate does not even consider the murder of himself as mistreatment, but can say: "Father, forgive them." They are identical with himself, who suffers by their action; he is the aggressor as well as the victim. Such is the true Spiritual Baptism of the Christian Mystic, and any other baptism that does not produce this universal fellow feeling is not worthy of the name.

CHAPTER THREE

THE TEMPTATION

We often hear about devout Christians complain of their periods
of depression. At times they are almost in the seventh heaven of
spiritual exaltation, they all but see the face of Christ and feel as if
He were guiding their every step; then without any warning and
without any cause that they can discover the clouds gather, the
Savior hides His face, and the world grows black for a period.
They cannot work, they cannot pray; the world has no attraction,
and the gate of heaven seems shut against them, with the result that
life appears worthless so long as this spiritual expression lasts. The
reason is, of course, that these people live in their emotions, and
under the immutable Law of Alternation the pendulum is bound to
swing as far to one side of the neutral point as it has swung to the
other. The brighter the light, the deeper the shadow, and the greater
the exaltation, the deeper the depression of spirit which follows it.
Only those who by cold reason restrain their emotions escape the
periods of depression, but they never taste the heavenly bliss of
exaltation either. AND IT IS THIS EMOTIONAL OUTPOURING
OF HIMSELF WHICH FURNISHED THE CHRISTIAN MYS-
TIC WITH THE DYNAMIC ENERGY TO PROJECT HIMSELF
INTO THE INVISIBLE WORLDS, WHERE HE BECOMES
ONE WITH THE SPIRITUAL IDEAL WHICH HAS BECK-
ONED HIM ON AND AWAKENED IN HIS SOUL THE
POWER TO RISE TO IT, as the sun built the eye wherewith we
perceive it. The nestling takes many a tumble ere it learns to use its
wings with assurance, and the aspirant upon the path of Christian
Mysticism may soar to the very throne of God times out of number
and then fall to the lowest pit of hell's despair. But some time he
will overcome the world, defy the Law of Alternation, and rise by
the power of the Spirit to the Father of Spirits, free from the toils

of emotion, filled with the peace that passeth understanding.

But that is the end attained only after Golgotha and the Mystic Baptism, the latter of which we discussed in the preceding chapter. Moreover, it is only the beginning of the active career of the Christian Mystic, in which he becomes thoroughly saturated with the tremendous fact of the unity of all life, and imbued with a fellow feeling for all creatures to such an extent that henceforth he can not only enunciate but practice the tenets of the Sermon on the Mount.

Did the spiritual experiences of the Christian Mystic take him no further, it would still be the most wonderful adventure in the world, and the magnitude of the event is beyond words, the consequences only dimly imaginable. Most students of the higher philosophies believe in the brotherhood of man from the mental conviction that we have all emanated from the same source, as rays emanate from the sun. But there is an abyss of inconceivable depth and width between this cold intellectual conception and the baptismal saturation of the Christian Mystic, who feels it is his heart and in every fiber of his being with such an intensity that it is actually painful to him; it fills him with such a yearning, aching love as that expressed in the words of the Christ: "Jerusalem, Jerusalem, how often would I have gathered thy children together, even as a hen gathereth her chickens under her wings;" a brooding, yearning, and achingly protective love which asks nothing for self save only the privilege to nurture, to shield, and to cherish.

Were even a faint resemblance to such a universal fellow feeling abroad among humanity in this dark day, what a paradise earth would be. Instead of every man's hand being against his brother to slay with the sword, with rivalry and competition, or to destroy his morals and degrade him by prison stripes or industrial bondage under the whiplash of necessity, we should have neither warriors nor prisoners but a happy contented world, living in peace and harmony, learning the lessons which our Father in Heaven aims to teach us in this material condition. AND ALL THE MISERY IN THE WORLD MAY BE ACCOUNTED FOR BY THE FACT

THAT IF WE BELIEVE IN THE BIBLE AT ALL, WE BELIEVE
WITH OUR HEAD AND NOT WITH OUR HEART.

When we came up through the waters of Baptism, the Atlantean
Flood, into the Rainbow Age of alternating seasons, we became
prey to the changing emotions which whirl us hither and yon upon
the sea of life. The cold faith restrained by reason entertained by
the majority of professing Christians may given them a need of
patience and mental valance which bears them up under the trials
of life, but when the majority get the LIVING FAITH of the Christian Mystic which laughs at reason because it is HEART-FELT,
then the Age of Alternation will be past, the rainbow will fall with
the clouds and the air which now composes the atmosphere, and
there will be a new heaven of pure ether, where we shall receive
the Baptism of Spirit and "THERE SHALL BE PEACE" (Jerusalem).

We are still in the Rainbow Age and subject to its low, so we
may realize that as the Baptism of the Christian Mystic occurs at a
time of spiritual exaltation, it must necessarily be followed by a
reaction. The tremendous magnitude of the revelation overpowers
him, he cannot realize it or contain it in his fleshly vehicle, so he
flees the haunts of men and betakes himself to the solitude alle-
gorically represented as a desert. So rapt is he in his sublime discovery that for the time being in his ecstasy he sees the Loom of
Life upon which the bodies of all that live are woven, from the
least to the greatest-the mouse and the man, the hunter and his
prey, the warrior and his victim. But to him they are not separate
and apart, for he also beholds the one divine thread of golden life-
light "which runs through all and doth all unite." Nay, more, he
hears in each the flaming keynote sounding its aspirations and
voicing its hopes and fears, and he perceives this composite color-
sound as the world anthem of God made flesh. This is at first entirely beyond his comprehension; the tremendous magnitude of the
discovery hides it from him, and he cannot conceive what it is that
he sees and feels, for there are no words to describe it, and no concept can cover it. But by degrees it dawns upon him that HE IS AT

THE VERY FOUNTAIN OF LIFE, beholding, nay, more, FEEL-ING its every pulse beat, and with this comprehension he reaches the climax of his ecstasy.

So rapt has the Christian Mystic been in his beautiful adventure that bodily wants have been completely forgotten till the ecstasy has passed, and it is therefore only natural that the feeling of hunger should be his first conscious want upon his return to the normal state of consciousness; and also naturally comes the voice of temptation: "COMMAND THAT THESE STONES BE MADE BREAD."

Few passages of the sacred Scriptures are darker that the opening verses of the Gospel of St. John: "In the beginning was the word . . . .and without it was not anything made that was made." A slight study of the science of sound soon makes us familiar with the fact that sound is vibration and that different sounds will mold sand or other light materials into figures of varying form. The Christian Mystic may be entirely ignorant of this fact from the scientific point of view, but he has learned at the Fountain of Life to sing the SONG OF BEING, which cradles into existence whatever such a master musician desires. There is one basic key for the indigestible mineral stone, but a modification will turn it to gold wherewith to purchase the means of sustenance, and another keynote peculiar to the vegetable kingdom will turn it into food, a fact known to all advanced occultists who practice incantations legitimately for spiritual purposes but never for material profit.

But the Christian Mystic who has just emerged from his Baptism in the Fountain of Life immediately shrinks in horror at the suggestion of using his newly discovered power for a selfish purpose. It was the very soul quality of unselfishness that ld him to the waters of consecration in the Fountain of life, and sooner would he sacrifice all, even life itself, that use this new-found power to spare himself a pang of pain. Did he not see also the Woe of the World? And does he not feel it in his great hearth with such an intensity that the hunger at once disappears and is forgotten? He may, will, and does use this wonderful power freely to feed the thousands that gather to hear him, but never for selfish purposes else he would upset the equilibrium of the world.

The Christian Mystic does not reason this out, however. As often stated, he has not reason, but he has a much safer guide in the interior voice which always speaks to him in moments when a decision must be made. "MAN DOES NOT LIVE BY BREAD ALONE, BUT BY EVERY WORD THAT PROCEEDETH FROM GOD";- another mystery. There is not need to partake of earthly bread for one who has access to the Fountain of Life. The more our thoughts are centered in God, the less we shall care for the so-called pleasures of the table, and by feeding our gross bodies sparingly on selected simple foods we shall obtain an illumination of spirit impossible to one who indulges in an excessive diet of coarse foods which nourish the lower nature. Some of the saints have used fasting and castigation as a means of soul growth, but that is a mistaken method for reasons given in an article on "Fasting for Soul Growth" published in the December 1915 number of "Rays from the Rose Cross." The Elder Brothers of humanity who understand the Law and live accordingly use food only at intervals measured by years. The word of God is to them a "living bread." So it becomes also to the Christian Mystic, and the Temptation instead of working his downfall has led him to greater heights.

CHAPTER FOUR

THE TRANSFIGURATION

We remember that by the mystic processes of the true Spiritual Baptism the aspirant becomes so thoroughly saturated with the Universal Spirit that as a matter of actual fact, feeling, and experience he becomes one with all that lives, moves, and has its being, one with the pulsating divine Life which surges in rhythmic cadence through the least and the greatest alike; and having caught the keynote of the celestial song he is then endued with a power of tremendous magnitude, which he may use either for good or ill. It should be understood and remembered that though gunpowder and dynamite facilitate farming when used for blowing up tree stumps which would otherwise require a great deal of manual labor to extract, they may also be used for destructive purposes as in the great European war. Spiritual powers also may be used for good or ill depending upon the motive and character of the one who wields them. Therefore, whoever has successfully undergone the rite of Baptism and thereby acquired spiritual power is forthwith tempted that it may be concerned decided whether he will range himself upon the side of good or evil. At this point he becomes either a future "Parsifal," a "Christ," a "Herod," or a "Klingsor" who fights the Knights of the Holy Grail with all the powers and resources of the Black Brotherhood.

There is a tendency in modern materialistic science to repudiate as fable, worthy of attention only among superstitious servant girls and foolish old women, the ideas commonly believed in as late as the Middle Ages, that such spiritual communities as the Knights of the Grail at one time existed, or that there are such beings as the "Black Brothers." Occult societies in the last half century have educated thousands to the fact that the Good Brothers are still in evidence and may be found by those who seek them in the proper way. Now unfortunately the tendency among this class of people is to accept anyone on his unsupported claims as a Master or an dept. But even among this class there are few who take the existence of the Black Brothers seriously, or realize what an enormous amount of damage they are doing in the world, and how they are aided and abetted by the general tendency of humanity to cater to the lusts of the flesh. As the good forces, which are symbolized as the servants of the Holy Grail, live and grow by unselfish service which enhances the luster of the glowing Grail Cup, so the Powers of Evil, known as the Black Grail and represented in the Bible as the court of Herod, feed on pride and sensuality, voluptuousness and passion, embodied in the figure of Salome, who glories in the murder of John the Baptist and the innocents. It was shown in the legend of the Grail as embodied in Wagner's "Parsifal" that when the Knights were denied the inspiration from the Grail Cup, on which they fed and which spurred them onto deeds of greater love and service, their courage flagged and they became inert. Similarly with the Brothers of the Black Grail. Unless they are provided with words of wickedness they will die from starvation. Therefore they are ever active in the world stirring up strife and inciting others to evil.

Were not this pernicious activity counteracted in a great measure by the Elder Brothers at their midnight services at which they make themselves magnets for all the evil thoughts in the Western World and then by the alchemy of sublime love transmute them to good, a cataclysm of still greater magnitude that the recent World War would have occurred long ago. As it is, the Genius of Evil has been held within bounds in some measure at least. Were humanity not so ready to range itself on the side of evil, success would have been greater. But it is hoped that the spiritual awakening started by the war will result in turning the scale and give the construction agencies in evolution the upper hand.

It is a wonderful power which is centered in the Christian Mystic at the time of his Baptism by the descent and concentration within him of the Universal Spirit; and when he has refused during the period of temptation to desecrate it for personal profit or power, he must of necessity give it vent in another direction, for he is impelled by an irresistible inner urge which will not allow him to settle down to an inert, inactive life of prayer and meditation. The power of God is upon him to preach and glad tidings to humanity, to help and heal. We know that a stove which is filled with burning fuel cannot help heating the surrounding atmosphere; neither can the Christian Mystic help radiating the divine compassion which fills his heart to overflowing, nor is he is doubt whom to love or whom to serve or where to find his opportunity. As the stove filled with burning fuel radiates heat to all who are within its sphere of radiation, so the Christian Mystic feels the love of God burning within his heart and is continually radiating it to all with whom he comes in contact. As the heated stove draws to itself by its genial warmth those who are suffering with physical cold, so the warm love rays of the Christian Mystic are as a magnet to all those whose hearts are chilled by the cruelty of the world, by man's inhumanity to man.

If the stove were empty but endowed with the faculty of speech, it might preach forever the gospel of warmth to those who are physically cold, but even the finest oratory would fail to satisfy its audience. When it has been filled with fuel and radiates warmth, there will be no need of preaching. Men will come to it and be satisfied. Similarly a sermon on brotherhood by one who has not laved in the "Fountain of Life" will sound hollow. The true Mystic need not preach. His every act, even his silent presence, is more powerful that all the most deeply thought-out discourses of learned doctors of philosophy.

There is a story of St. Francis of Assisi which particularly illustrates this fact, and which we trust may serve to drive it home, for its exceedingly important. It is said that one day St. Francis went to a young brother in the monastery with which he was then connected and said to him: "Brother, let us go down to the village and preach to them." The young brother was naturally overjoyed at the honor and opportunity of accompanying so hold a man as St. Francis, and together the two started toward the village, talking all the while about spiritual things and the life that leads to God. Engrossed in this conversation they passed through the village, walking along its various streets, now and then stopping to speak a kindly word to one or another of the villagers. After having made a circuit of the village St. Francis was heading toward the road which led to the monastery when of a sudden the young brother reminded him of his intention to preach in the village and asked him if he had forgotten it. To this St. Francis answered: "My son, are you not aware that all the while we have been in this village we have been preaching to the people all around us? In the first place, our simple dress proclaims the fact that we are devoted to the service of God, and as soon as anyone sees us his thoughts naturally turn heavenward. Be sure that everyone of the villagers has been watching us, taking note of our demeanor to see in how far it conforms with our profession. They have listened to our words to find whether they were about spiritual or profane subjects. They have watched our gestures and have noted that the words of sympathy we dispensed came straight from our hearts and went deep into theirs. We have been preaching a far more powerful sermon that if we had gone into the market place, called them around us, and started to harangue them with an exhortation to holiness."

St. Francis was a Christian Mystic in the deepest sense of the word, and being taught from within by the spirit of God he knew well the mysteries of life, as did Jacob Boehme and other holy men who have been similarly taught. They are in a certain sense wiser than the wisest of the intellectual school, but it is not necessary for them to expound great mysteries in order to fulfill their mission and serve as guide posts to others who are also seeking God. The very simplicity of their words and acts carries with it the power of conviction. Naturally, of course, all do not rise to the same heights. All have not the same powers anymore than all the stoves are of the same size and have the same heating capacity. Those who follow the Christian Mystic path, from the least to the greatest, have experienced the powers conveyed by Baptism according to their capacity. They have been tempted to use those powers in an evil direction for personal gain, and having overcome the desire for the world and worldly things they have turned to the path of ministry and service as Christ did; their lives are marked not so much by what they have said as by what they have done. The true Christian Mystic is easily distinguished. He never uses the six week days to prepare for a grand oratorical effort to thrill his hearers on Sunday, but spends every day alike in humble endeavor to do the Master's will regardless of outward applause. Thus unconsciously he works up toward that grand climax which in the history of the noblest of all who have trod this path is spoken of as the "Transfiguration."

The Transfiguration is an alchemical process by which the physical body formed by the chemistry of physiological processes is turned into a living stone such as is mentioned in the Bible. The medieval alchemists who were seeking the Philosopher's Stone were not concerned with transmutation of such dross as material god, but aimed at the greater goal as indicated above.

Moisture gathered in the clouds falls to earth as rain when it has condensed sufficiently, and it is again evaporated into clouds by the heat of the sun. This is the primal cosmic formula. Spirit also condenses itself into matter and becomes mineral. But though it be crystallized into the harness of flint, life still remains, and by the alchemy of nature working through another life stream the dense mineral constituents of the soil are transmuted to a more flexible structure in the plant, which may be used as food for animal and man. These substances become sentient flesh by the alchemy of assimilation. When we note the changes in the structure of the human body evidenced by comparison of the Bushmen, Chinese, Hindus, Latins, Celts, and Anglo-Saxons, it is plainly apparent that the flesh of man is even now undergoing a refining process which is eradicating the coarser, grosser substances. In time by evolution this process of spiritualization will render our flesh transparent and radiant with the Light that shines within, radiant as the face of Moses, the body of Buddha, and the Christ at the Transfiguration.

At present the effulgence of the indwelling Spirit is effectually darkened by our dense body, but we may draw hop even from the science of chemistry. There is nothing on earth so rare and precious as radium, the luminous extract of the dense black mineral called pitchblende; and there is nothing so rare as that precious extract of the human body, the radiant Christ. At present we are laboring to form the Christ within, but when the inner Christ has grown to full stature, He will shine through the transparent body as the LIGHT OF THE WORLD.

It is an anatomical fact of common knowledge that the spinal cord is divided into three sections, from which the motor, sensory, and sympathetic nerves are controlled. Astrologically these are ruled by the moon, Mars, and Mercury, which are divine Hierarchies that have played a great role in human evolution through the nervous systems indicated. Among the ancient alchemists these were designated by the three alchemical elements, salt, sulphur, and mercury. Between them and upon them played the spinal Spirit Fire of Neptune. It rose in a serpentine column through the spinal cord to the ventricles of the brain. In the great majority of mankind the Spirit Fire is still exceedingly weak. But whenever a spiritual awakening occurs in anyone such as that which takes place in a genuine conversion, or better still at the Baptism of the Christian Mystic, the downpouring of the Spirit, which is an actual fact, augments the spinal Spirit Fire to an almost unbelievable extent, and forthwith a process of regeneration begins whereby the gross substances of the threefold body of many are gradually thrown out, rendering the vehicles more permeable and quickly responsive to spiritual impulses. The further the process if carried, the more efficient servants they become in the vineyard of the Master.

The spiritual awakening which starts this process of regeneration in the Christian Mystic who purifies himself by prayer and service, comes also of course to those who are seeking God by way of knowledge and service, but it acts in a different way, which is noted by the spiritual investigator. In the Christian Mystic the regenerative spinal Spirit Fire is concentrated principally upon the lunar segment of the spinal cord, which governs the sympathetic nerves under the rulership of Jehovah. Therefore his spiritual

70

growth is accomplished by faith as simple, childlike, and unquestioning as it was in the days of early Atlantis when men were mindless. He therefore draws down the great white Light of Deity reflected through Jehovah, the Holy Spirit, and attains to the whole wisdom of the world without the necessity of laboring for it intellectually. This gradually transmutes his body into THE WHITE PHILOSOPHER'S STONE, THE DIAMOND SOUL.

In those, on the other hand, whose minds are strong and insistent on knowing the reason why and the wherefore of every dictum and dogma, the Spinal Fire of regeneration plays upon the segments of the red Mars and the colorless Mercury, endeavoring to infuse desire with reason, to purify the former of the primal passion that it may become chaste as the rose, and thus transmute the body into the RUBY SOUL, THE RED PHILOSOPHER'S STONE, TRIED BY FIRE, PURIFIED, A CREATIVE BUDDING INDIVIDUALITY.

All who are upon the Path, whether the path of occultism or of mysticism, are weaving the "golden wedding garment" by this work from within and from without. In some the gold is exceedingly pale, and in others it is deeply red. But eventually when the process of Transfiguration has been completed, or rather when it is nearing completion, the extremes will blend, and the transfigured bodies will become balanced in color, for the occultist must learn the lesson of deep devotion, and the Christian Mystic must learn how to acquire knowledge by his own efforts without drawing upon the universal source of all wisdom.

This view gives us a deeper insight into the Transfiguration reported in the Gospels. We should remember distinctly that IT WAS THE VEHICLES OF JESUS WHICH WERE TRANSFIGURED temporarily by the indwelling Christ Spirit. But even while allowing for the enormous potency of the Christ Spirit in effecting the Transfiguration it is evident that Jesus must be a sublime character without a peer. The Transfiguration as seen in the Memory of Nature reveals his body as a dazzling white, thus showing his dependence upon the Father, the Universal Spirit. There is a great diversity in present attainments, but in the kingdom of Christ the differences will gradually disappear, and a uniform color indicating both knowledge and devotion will be acquired by all. This color will correspond to the pink color seen by occultists as the Spiritual Sun, the vehicle of the Father. When this has been accomplished, the Transfiguration of humanity will be complete. We shall then be one with our Father, and His kingdom will have come.

CHAPTER FIVE

THE LAST SUPPER AND THE FOOTWASHING

We are told in the Gospels which relate the story of the Christian Mystic Initiation, how on the night when Christ had partaken of the Last Supper with His disciples, His ministry being finished at that time, He rose from the table and girded Himself with a towel, then poured water into a basin and commenced to wash His disciples' feet, an act of the most humble service, but prompted by an important occult consideration.

Comparatively few realize that when we rise in the scale of evolution, we do so by trampling upon the bodies of our weaker brothers; consciously or unconsciously we crush them and use them as stepping-stones to attain our own ends. This assertion holds good concerning all the kingdoms in nature. When a life wave has been brought down to the nadir of involution and encrusted in mineral form, that is immediately seized upon by another slightly higher life wave, which takes the disintegrating mineral crystal, adapts it to its own ends as crystalloid, and assimilates it as part of a plant form. If there were no minerals which could thus be seized upon, disintegrated, and transformed, plant life would be an impossibility. Then again, the plant forms are taken by numerous classes of animals, masticated to a pulp, devoured, and made to serve as food for this higher kingdom. If there were no plants, animals would be an impossibility; and the same principle holds good in spiritual evolution for if there were no pupils standing on the lower round of the ladder of knowledge and requiring instruction, there would be no need for a teacher. But here there is one all-important difference. The teacher grows by GIVING to his pupils and serving them. From their shoulders he steps to a higher rung on the ladder of knowledge. HE LIFTS HIMSELF BY LIFTING THEM, but nevertheless he owes them a debt of gratitude, which is symbolically acknowledged and liquidated by the foot washing--an act of humble service to those who have served him.

When we realize that nature, which is the expression of God, is continually exerting itself to create and bring forth, we may also understand that whoever kills anything, be it ever so little and seemingly insignificant, is to that extent thwarting God's purpose. This applies particularly to the aspirant to the higher life, and therefore the Christ exhorted His disciples to be wise as serpents but harmless as doves notwithstanding. But no matter how earnest our desire to follow the precept of harmlessness, our constitutional tendencies and necessities force us to kill at every moment of our lives, and it is not only in the great things that we are constantly committing murder. It was comparatively easy for the seeking soul symbolized by Parsifal to break the bow wherewith he had shot the swan of the Grail knights when it had been explained to him what a wrong he had committed. From that time Parsifal was committed to the life of harmlessness so far as the great things were concerned. All earnest aspirants follow him readily in that act once it has dawned upon them how subversive of soul growth is the practice of partaking of food which requires the death of an animal.

But even the noblest and most gentle among mankind is poisoning those about him with every breath and being poisoned by them in turn, for all exhale the death-dealing carbon dioxide, and we are therefore a menace to one another. Nor is this a far-fetched idea; it is a very real danger which will become much more manifest in course of time when mankind becomes more sensitive. In a disabled submarine or under similar conditions where a number of people are together the carbon dioxide exhaled by them quickly makes the atmosphere unable to sustain life. There is a story from the Indian Mutiny of how a number of English prisoners were huddled in a room in which there was only one small opening for air. In a very short time the oxygen was exhausted, and the poor prisoners began to fight one another like beasts in order to obtain a place near that air inlet, and they fought until nearly all had died from the struggle and asphyxiation.

The same principle is illustrated in the ancient Atlantean Mystery Temple, the Tabernacle in the Wilderness, where we find a nauseating stench and a suffocating smoke ascending from the Altar of Burnt Offerings, where the poison-laden bodies of the UNWILLING VICTIMS sacrificed for sin were consumed, and where the light shone but dimly through the enveloping smoke. This we may contrast with the light which emanated clear and bright from the Seven-branched Candlestick fed by the olive oil extracted from the chaste plant, and where the incense symbolized by the WILLING SERVICE of devoted priests rose to heaven as a sweet savor. This we are told in many places, was pleasing to Deity, while the blood of the unwilling victims, the bulls and the goats, was a source of grief and displeasure to God, who delights most in the sacrifice of prayer, which helps the devotee and harms no one.

It has been stated concerning some of the saints that they emitted a sweet odor, and as we have often had occasion to say, this is no mere fanciful story--it is an occult fact. The great majority of mankind inhale during every moment of life the vitalizing oxygen contained in the surrounding atmosphere. At every expiration we exhale a charge of carbon dioxide which is a deadly poison and which would certainly vitiate the air in time if the pure and chaste plant did not inhale this poison, use a part of it to build bodies that last sometimes for many centuries or even millennia as instanced in the redwoods of California, and give us back the rest in the form of pure oxygen which we need for our life. These carboniferous plant bodies by certain further processes of nature have in the past become mineralized and turned to stone instead of disintegrating. We find them today as coal, THE PERISHABLE PHILOSOPHER'S STONE MADE BY NATURAL MEANS IN NATURE'S LABORATORY. But the Philosopher's Stone may also be made artificially by man from his own body. It should be understood once and for all that the Philosopher's Stone is not made in an exterior chemical laboratory, but that the body is the workshop of the Spirit which contains all the elements necessary to produce this ELIXIR VITAE, and that the Philosopher's Stone is not exterior to the body, but THE ALCHEMIST HIMSELF BECOMES THE

PHILOSOPHER'S STONE. The salt, sulphur, and mercury emblematically contained in the three segments of the spinal cord, which control the sympathetic, motor, and sensory nerves and are played upon by the Neptunian spinal Spirit Fire, constitute the essential elements in the alchemical process.

It needs no argument to show that indulgence in sensuality, brutality, and bestiality makes the body coarse. Contrariwise, devotion to Deity, an attitude of perpetual prayer, a feeling of love and compassion for all that lives and moves, loving thoughts sent out to all beings and those inevitably received in return, all invariably have the effect of refining and spiritualizing the nature. We speak of a person of that sort as breathing or radiating love, an expression which much more nearly describes the actual fact than most people imagine, for as a matter of actual observation the percentage of poison contained in the breath of an individual is in exact proportion to the evil in his nature and inner life and the thoughts he thinks. The Hindu Yogi makes a practice of sealing up the candidate for a certain grade of Initiation in a cave which is not much larger than his body. There he must live for a number of weeks breathing the same air over and over again to demonstrate practically that he has ceased exhaling the death-dealing carbon dioxide and is beginning to build his body therefrom.

The Philosopher's Stone then is not a body of the same nature as the plant, thought it is pure and chaste, but it is A CELESTIAL BODY such as that whereof St. Paul speaks in the 5th chapter of Second Corinthians, a body which becomes immortal as a diamond or a ruby stone. It is not hard and inflexible as the mineral; it is A SOFT DIAMOND or ruby, and by every act of the nature described the Christian Mystic is building this body, though he is probably unconscious thereof for a long time. When he has attained to this degree of holiness it is not necessary for him to perform the foot washing so far as concerns the physical pupil who helps him to rise, but he will always have the feeling of gratitude, symbolized by that act, toward those whom he is fortunate enough to attract to himself as disciples and to whom he may give the living bread which nourishes them to immortality.

Students will realize that this is part of the process which eventually culminates in the Transfiguration, but it should also be realized that in the Christian Mystic Initiation there are no set and definite degrees. The candidate looks to the Christ as the author and finisher of his faith, seeking to imitate Him and follow in His steps through every moment of existence. Thus the various stages which we are considering are reached by processes of soul growth which simultaneously bring him to higher aspects of all these steps that we are now analyzing. In this respect the Christian Mystic Initiation differs radically from the processes in vogue among the Rosicrucians, in which an UNDERSTANDING upon the part of the candidate of that which is to take place is considered indispensable. But there comes a time at which the Christian Mystic must and does realize the path before him, and that is what constitutes Gethsemane, which we will consider in the next chapter.

CHAPTER SIX

GETHSEMANE

THE GARDEN OF GRIEF

And when they had sung a hymn, they went out into the Mount of Olives. "And Jesus saith unto them, All ye shall be offended because of me this night; for it is written, I will smite the Shepherd, and the sheep shall be scattered. But after that I am risen I will go before you into Galilee.

"But Peter said unto him, Although all shall be offended, yet will not I. "And Jesus saith unto him, Verily, I say unto thee that this day, even in this night, before the cock crow twice, thou shalt deny me thrice.

"But he spake the more vehemently, If I should die with thee, I will not deny thee in any wise. Likewise also said they all.

"And they came to a place which was named Gethsemane: and He saith to His disciples, Sit ye here while I shall pray. And He taketh with Him Peter and James and John, and began to be sore amazed, and to be very heavy; and saith unto them, My soul is exceedingly sorrowful unto death: tarry ye here and watch. And He went forward a little, and fell on the ground, and prayed that if it were possible the hour might pass from him. And He said, Abba, Father, all things are possible unto thee; take away this cup from me: Nevertheless, not what I will, but what thou wilt. And he cometh and findeth them sleeping, and saith unto Peter, Simon, sleepest thou? Couldst not thou watch one hour? Watch ye and pray lest ye enter into temptation. The spirit truly is ready, but the flesh is weak." --MARK, 14:26-38.

In the foregoing Gospel narrative we have one of the saddest and most difficult of the experiences of the Christian Mystic outlined in spiritual form. During all his previous experience he has wandered blindly along, that is to say, blind to the fact that he is on the Path which if consistently followed leads to a definite goal, but being also keenly alert to the slightest sigh of every suffering soul. He has concentrated all his efforts upon alleviating their pain physically, morally, or mentally; he has served them in any and every capacity; he has taught them the gospel of love, "Thou shalt love thy neighbor as thyself"; and he has been A LIVING EXAMPLE to all in its practice. Therefore he has drawn to himself a little band of friends whom he loves with the tenderest of affection. Them has he also taught and served unstintingly, even to the foot washing. But during this period of service he has become so saturated with the sorrows of the world that he is indeed a MAN of SORROWS and acquainted with grief as no one else can be.

This is a very definite experience of the Christian Mystic, and it is the most important factor in furthering his spiritual progress. So long as we are bored when people come to us and tell us their troubles, so long as we run away from them and seek to escape hearing their tales of woe, we are far from the Path. Even when we listen to them and have schooled ourselves not to show that we are bored, when we say with our lips only a few sympathetic words that fall flat on the sufferer's ear, we gain nothing in spiritual growth. It is absolutely essential to the Christian Mystic that he become so attuned to the world's woe that he feels every pang as his own hurt and stores it up within his heart.

When PARSIFAL stood in the temple of the Holy Grail and saw the suffering of Amfortas the stricken Grail King, he was mute with sympathy and compassion for a long time after the procession had passed out of the hall, and consequently could not answer the questions of Gurnemanz, and it was that deep fellow feeling which prompted him to seek for the spear that should heal Amfortas. IT WAS THE PAIN OF AMFORTAS FELT IN THE HEART OF PARSIFAL BY SYMPATHY WHICH HELD HIM FIRMLY BALANCED UPON THE PATH OF VIRTUE WHEN TEMP-

TATION WAS STRONGEST. It was that deep pain of compassion which urged him through many years to seek the suffering Grail King, and finally when he had found Amfortas, this deep, heartfelt fellow feeling enabled him to pour forth the healing balm.

As it is shown in the soul myth of Parsifal, so it is in the actual life and experience of the Christian Mystic: he must drink deeply of the cup of sorrow, he must drain it to the very dregs so that by the cumulative pain which threatens to burst his heart he may pour himself out unreservedly and unstintedly for the healing and helping of the world. Then Gethsemane, the garden of grief, is a familiar place to him, watered with tears for the sorrows and sufferings of humanity.

Through all his years of self-sacrifice his little band of friends had been the consolation of Jesus. He had already learned to renounce the ties of blood. "Who is my mother and my brother? They that do the will of my Father." Though no true Christian neglects his social obligations or withholds love from his family, the spiritual ties are nevertheless the strongest, and through them comes the crowning grief; through the desertion of his spiritual friends he learns to drink to the dregs the cup of sorrow. He does not blame them for their desertion but excuses them with the words, "The Spirit is indeed willing, but the flesh is weak," for he knows by his own experience how true this is. But he finds that in the supreme sorrow they cannot comfort him, and therefore he turns to THE ONLY SOURCE OF COMFORT, THE FATHER IN HEAVEN. He has arrived at the point where human endurance seems to have reached its limit, and he prays to be spared a greater ordeal, but with a blind trust in the Father he bows his will and offers all unreservedly.

That is the moment of realization. Having drunk the cup of sorrow to the dregs, being deserted by all, he experiences that temporary awful fear of being utterly alone which is one of the most terrible if not the most terrible experience that can come into the life of a human being. All the world seems dark about. He knows that in spite of all the good he has done or tried to do the powers of darkness are seeking to slay him. He knows that the mob that a few days before had cried "Hosanna" will on the morrow be ready to shout "Crucify! Crucify!" His relatives and now his last few friends have fled, and they were also even ready to deny.

But when we are on the pinnacle of grief we are nearest to the throne of grace. The agony and grief, the sorrow and the suffering borne within the Christian Mystic's breast are more priceless and precious than the wealth of the Indies, for when he has lost all human companionship and when he has given himself over unreservedly to the Father a transmutation takes place: the grief is turned to compassion, the only power in the world that can fortify a man about to mount the hill of Golgotha and give his life for humanity, not a sacrifice of death but a LIVING SACRIFICE, lifting himself by lifting others.

CHAPTER SEVEN

THE STIGMATA AND THE CRUCIFIXION

As we said in the beginning of this series of articles, the Christian Mystic Initiation differs radically from the Occult Initiation undertaken by those who approach the Path from the intellectual side. But all paths converge at Gethsemane, where the candidate for Initiation is saturated with sorrow which flowers into compassion, a yearning mother love which has only one all-absorbing desire; to pour itself out for the alleviation of the sorrow of the world to save and to succor all that are weak and heavy-laden, to comfort them and give them rest. At that point the eyes of the Christian Mystic are opened to a full realization of the world's woe and his mission as a Savior; and the occultist also finds here the heart of love which alone can give zest and zeal in the quest. By the union of the mind and the heart both are ready for the next step, which involved the development of the STIGMATA, a necessary preparation for the mystic death and resurrection. The Gospel narrative tells the story of the STIGMATA in the following words, the opening scene being in the Garden of Gethsemane:

"Judas then having received a band of men and officers from the chief priests and Pharisees came thither with lanterns, torches, and weapons. Jesus therefore knowing all things that should come upon Him went forth and said unto them, Whom seek ye? They answered Him, Jesus of Nazareth. Jesus said unto them, I am He.....Then the band and the captain and the officers of the Jews took Jesus and bound Him and led Him away to Annas first.....The high priest then asked of His disciples and of His doctrine. Jesus answered him, I spake openly to the world.....Why asketh though me? Ask them which heard me what I have said unto them; behold they know what I have said. Now Annas had sent Him bound unto Caiaphas the high priest.....Then they led Jesus from Caiaphas unto the hall of judgment.....

"Pilate then went out unto them and said, What accusation bring you against this man? They answered and said unto him, If He were not a malefactor we would not have delivered Him unto thee.....Then Pilate entered into the judgment hall again, and called Jesus, and said unto Him, Art though the King of the Jews? Jesus answered him, Sayest thou this thing of thyself or did others tell it to thee of me?.....My kingdom is not of this world: if my kingdom were of this world, then would my servants fight that I should not be delivered to the Jews; but now is my kingdom not from hence. Pilate therefore said unto him, Art thou a king then? Jesus answered, Thou sayest that I am a king. To this end was I born, and for this cause came I into the world that I should bear witness unto the truth. Everyone that is of the truth heareth my voice. Pilate said unto Him, What is truth?.....Then he went out again unto the Jews and saith unto them, I find in Him no fault at all. But we have a custom that I should release unto you one at the Passover; will ye therefore that I release unto you the King of the Jews? Then cried they all again saying, Not this man, but Barabbas. now Barabbas was a robber. Pilate therefore took Jesus and SCOURGED Him. And the soldiers platted A CROWN OF THORNS and put it on His head, and they put on Him a purple robe and said, Hail, King of the Jews; and they smote him with their hands.

"Pilate therefore went forth again and saith unto them, behold I bring Him forth unto you that ye may know that I find no fault in Him. Then came Jesus forth wearing the crown of thorns and the purple robe. And Pilate saith unto them, Behold the man! When the chief priests therefore, and officers saw Him, they cried out, saying, Crucify Him, Crucify Him. Pilate saith unto them, Take ye Him and crucify Him; for I find no fault in Him. The Jews answered him, We have a law and by our law He ought to die, because He made Himself the Son of God.....Pilate sought to release Him, but the Jews cried out saying, If thou let this man go, thou art not Caesar's friend; whoever maketh himself a king speaketh against Caesar.....They cried out, Away with Him, away with Him, crucify Him. Pilate saith unto them, Shall I crucify your king? The chief priests answered, We have no king but Caesar. Then delivered he Him therefore unto them to be crucified. And they took Jesus and led Him away. And He, bearing His cross, went forth into a place called the PLACE OF A SKULL, which is, in the Hebrew, Golgotha. There they CRUCIFIED Him and two others with Him, one on either side and Jesus in the midst. And Pilate wrote a title and put it on the cross. And the writing was, JESUS OF NAZARETH, THE KING OF THE JEWS."

We have here the account of how the STIGMATA or punctures were produced in the Hero of the Gospels, though the location is not quite correctly described, and the process is represented in a narrative form differing widely from the manner in which these things really happen. But we stand here before one of the Mysteries which must remain sealed for the profane, though the underlying mystical facts are as plain as daylight to those who know. The physical body is not by any means the real man. Tangible, solid, and pulsating with life as we find it, it is really the most dead part of the human being, crystallized into a matrix of finer vehicles which are invisible to our ordinary physical sight. If we place a basin of water in a freezing temperature, the water soon congeals into ice, and when we examine this ice, we find that it is made up of innumerable little crystals having various geometrical forms and lines of demarcation. There are etheric lines of forces which were present in the water before it congealed. As the water was hardened and molded along these lines, so our physical bodies have congealed and solidified along the etheric lines of force of our invisible vital body, which is thus in the ordinary course of life inextricably bound to the physical body, waking or sleeping, until death brings dissolution of the tie. But as Initiation involves the liberation of the REAL MAN from the body of sin and death that he may soar into the subtler spheres at will and return to the body at his pleasure, it is obvious that before that can be accomplished, before the object of Initiation can be attained, the interlocking grip of the physical body and the etheric vehicle which is so strong and rigid in ordinary humanity, must be dissolved. As they are most closely bound together in the palms of the hands, the arches of the feet, and the head, the occult schools concentrate their efforts upon severing the connection at these points, and produce the STIGMATA invisibly.

The Christian Mystic lacks knowledge of how to perform the act without producing an exterior manifestation. The STIGMATA develop in him spontaneously by constant contemplation of Christ and unceasing efforts to imitate Him in all things. These exterior STIGMATA comprise not only the wounds in the hands and feet and that in the side but also those impressed by the crown of thorns and by the scourging. The most remarkable example of stigmatization is that said to have occurred in 1224 to Francis of Assisi on the mountain of Alverno. Being absorbed in contemplation of the Passion he saw a seraph approaching, blazing with fire and having between its wings the figure of the Crucified. St. Francis became aware that in hands, feet, and side he had received externally the marks of crucifixion. These marks continued during the two years until his death, and are claimed to have been seen by many eyewitnesses, including Pope Alexander the Fourth.

The Dominicans disputed the fact, but at length made the same claim for Catherine of Sienna, whose STIGMATA were explained as having at her own request been made invisible to others. The Franciscans appealed to Sixtus the Fourth who forbade representation of St. Catherine to made with the STIGMATA. Still the fact of the STIGMATA is recorded in the Breviary Office, and Benedict the 13th granted the Dominicans a Feast in commemoration of it. Others, especially women who have the positive vital body, are claimed to have received some or all of the STIGMATA. The last to be canonized by the Catholic Church for this reason was Veronica Giuliana (1831). More recent cases are those of Anna Catherine Emmerich, who became a nun at Agnetenberg; L'Estatica Maria Von Moerl of Caldero; Louise Lateau, whose STIGMATA were said to bleed every Friday; and Mrs. Girling of the Newport Shaker community.

But whether the STIGMATA are visible or invisible the effect is the same. The spiritual currents generated in the vital body of such a person are so powerful that the body is scourged by them as it were, particularly in the region of the head, where they produce a feeling akin to that of the crown of thorns. Thus there finally dawns upon the person a full realization that the physical body is a cross which he is bearing, a prison and not the real man. This brings him to the next step in his Initiation, viz., the crucifixion, which is experienced by the development of the other centers in his hands and feet where the vital body is thus being severed from the dense vehicle.

We are told in the Gospel story that Pilate placed a sign reading, 'JESUS NAZARENUS REX JUDAEOREM" on Jesus' cross, and this is translated in the authorized version to mean, "Jesus of Nazareth the King of the Jews." But the initials INRI placed upon the cross represent the names of the four elements in Hebrew: IAM, water; NOUR, fire; RUACH, spirit or vital air; and IABESHAH, earth. This is the occult key to the mystery of crucifixion, for it symbolizes in the first place the salt, sulphur, mercury, and azoth which were used by the ancient alchemists to make the Philosopher's Stone, the universal solvent, the ELIXIR-VITAE. The two "I's" (IAM and IABESHAH) represent the saline lunar water: a, in a fluidic state holding salt in solution, and b, the coagulated extract of this water, the "SALT OF THE EARTH"; in other words, the finer fluidic vehicles of man and his dense body. N (NOUR) in Hebrew stands for fire and the combustible elements, chief among which are SULPHUR and PHOSPHORUS so necessary to oxidation, without which warm blood would be an impossibility. The Ego under this condition could not function in the body nor could thought find a material expression. R (RUACH) is the Hebrew equivalent for the spirit, AZOTH, functioning in the MERCURIAL mind. Thus the four letters INRI placed over the cross of Christ according to the Gospel story represent composite man, the Thinker, at the point in his spiritual development where he is getting ready for liberation from the cross of his dense vehicle.

Proceeding further along the same line of elucidation we may note that INRI is the symbol of the crucified candidate for the following additional reasons:

IAM is the Hebrew word signifying water, the fluidic LUNAR, moon element which forms the principal part of the human body (about 87 per cent). This word is also the symbol of the finer fluidic vehicles of desire and emotion. NOUR, the Hebrew word signifying fire, is a symbolic representation of the heat-producing red blood laden with martial Mars iron, fire, and energy, which the occultist sees coursing as a gas through the veins and arteries of the human body infusing it with energy and ambition without which there could be neither material nor spiritual progress. It also represents the sulphur and phosphorus necessary for the material manifestation of thought as already mentioned.

RUACH, the Hebrew word for spirit or vital air, is an excellent symbol of the Ego clothed in the mercurial Mercury mind, which makes MAN and enables him to control and direct his bodily vehicles and activities in a rational manner.

IABESHAH is the Hebrew word for earth, representing the solid fleshy part which makes up the CRUCIFORM EARTHY BODY crystallized within the finer vehicles at birth and severed from them in the ordinary course of things at death, or in the extraordinary event that we learn to die the mystic death and ascend to the glories of the higher spheres for a time.

This stage of the Christian Mystic's spiritual development therefore involves a reversal of the creative force from its ordinary downward course where it is wasted in generation to satisfy the passions, to an upward course through the tripartite spinal cord, whose three segments are ruled by the moon, Mars, and Mercury respectively, and where the rays of Neptune then lights THE RE-GENERATIVE SPINAL SPIRIT FIRE. This mounting upward sets the pituitary body and the pineal gland into vibration, opening up the spiritual sight; and striking the frontal sinus it starts the

CROWN OF THORNS throbbing with pain as the bond with the physical body is burned by the sacred Spirit Fire, which wakes this center from its age-long sleep to a throbbing, pulsating life sweeping onward to the other centers in the FIVE-POINTED STIGMATIC STAR. They are also vitalized, an the whole vehicle becomes aglow with a golden glory. Then with a final wrench the great vortex of the desire body located in the liver is liberated, and the martial energy contained in that vehicle propels upward the SIDEREAL VEHICLE (so- called because the STIGMATA in the head, hands, and feet are located in the same positions relative to one another as the points in a five-pointed star), which ascends through THE SKULL (Golgotha), while the CRUCIFIED CHRISTIAN utters his triumphant cry, "Consummatum est" (it has been accomplished), and soars into the subtler spheres to seek Jesus whose life he has imitated with such success and from whom he is thenceforth inseparable. Jesus is his Teacher and his guide to the kingdom of Christ, where all shall be united in one body to learn and to practice the RELIGION OF THE FATHER, to whom the kingdom will eventually revert that He may be All in All.

The Bonseigneur Rituals
Edited by Gerry L. Prinsen
Foreword by Michael R. Poll

8x10 Softcover 2 volumes 574 pages
Retail Price: $54.95
ISBN 1-934935-34-4

This work is a rare collection of 18th century New Orleans Ecossais Masonic Rituals. Included are a photographic reproduction of the original handwritten French ritual, a French transcription and English translation.
The work provides a valuable link in the understanding of the development of both Louisiana Masonry as well as the Ancient and Accepted Scottish Rite. This collection is indispensable to any serious study of early Masonic rituals. Two volume set.

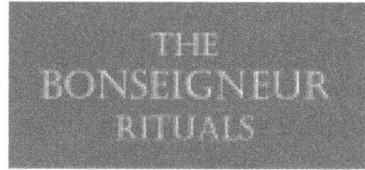

More Light - Masonic Enlightenment
Series
Edited by Michael R. Poll
6 x 9 Softcover 194 pages
Retail Price: $16.95
ISBN 1-934935-36-0

This is the a follow-up to the popular book "Masonic Englightenment." Includes the inspired Masonic essays: "Mythology and Masonry" by R.J. Meekren; "Geometry of God" by Joseph Fort Newton; "The Suppression of the Order of the Temple" by Frederick W. Hamilton; "Was William Shakespeare a Freemason?" by Robert I. Clegg; "The Religion of Robert Burns" by Gilbert Patten Brown; "Hysteria in Freemasonry" by WM. F. Kuhn; "The Square and the Cross" by A.S. MacBride; "Toleration and Freethinking" by H.L. Haywood and more.

The Freemasons Key
Edited by Michael R. Poll
6 x 9 Softcover 244 pages
Retail Price: $18.95
ISBN 1-88756-097-1

Symbolism is the language of Freemasonry. But what is symbolism? Why does
Masonry use it? Who else has used symbolism? Some of the great minds in Masonic history (Albert Mackey, Joseph Fort
Newton, Oliver Day Street, H. L.
Haywood and more) answer these and
other questions concerning the Masonic
method of teaching as well as explain the symbolism of the Masonic
degrees. This is an indispensable work for anyone seeking to better
understand Freemasonry and its practices.

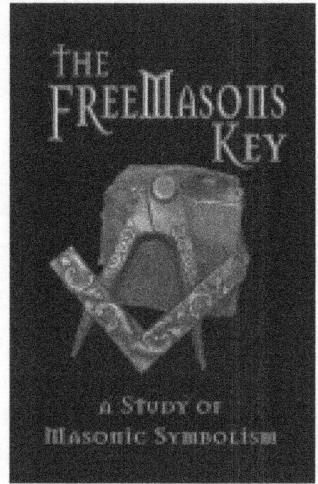

Review by Edward L. King

"Mike Poll has developed a keen sense of 'what's needed' in the publishing of
Masonic books. In this work, he's filled a HUGE gap that has existed practically
forever.

When one becomes a Mason, the very first thing they want to learn about is
'symbolism'. What does it all mean? What's behind it all? For several decades, the
standard work to address these emergent questions has been Allen Roberts' The
Craft and Its Symbols. This book will not take its place but it should easily become
the SECOND reference for a new or inquiring Masonic mind. While Roberts has
addressed the basics, relating them to each degree in a logical, patterned order, this
work expands FAR beyond that and joins together essays from the best and bright-
est minds from the history of Freemasonry into a book which expands the richness
of our symbolism in detail. Having these all in one easily handled volume makes it
just SO much easier!

This is not to say that these essays themselves are easy: they are, for the most
part, ones to which you will return again and again over the years, each time finding
new gems of thought-provoking stimulation. They approach the subject of Masonic symbolism from varying angles, allowing the rich prism to shine and glow in
your mind.

This is a book that has long been needed: I urge ANY student of Masonic
symbolism to add it to their 'read this now' list and to their library immediately."

Outline of the Rise and Progress of Freemasonry in Louisiana

by James B. Scot
Introduction by Alain Bernheim
Afterword by Michael R. Poll

8x10 Softcover 180 pages
Retail Price: $24.95
ISBN 1-934935-31-X

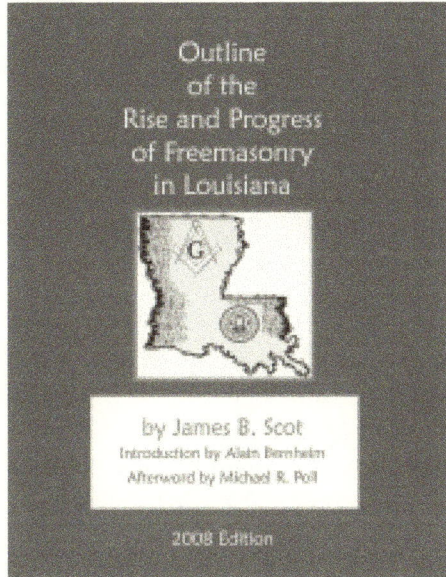

Outline
of the
Rise and Progress
of Freemasonry
in Louisiana

by James B. Scot
Introduction by Alain Bernheim
Afterword by Michael R. Poll

2008 Edition

This facsimile reproduction of the 1873 first edition is the granddaddy of modern Louisiana Masonic history books. Scot traces Louisiana Masonry from the organization of Perfect Union and Etoile Polaire Lodges until approximately 1870. Bitingly hostile remarks towards James Foulhouze (some taken from the works of Albert Pike) show the highly emotional climate of Louisiana Masonry in the late 1800's. While Scot sometimes allowed his emotions to get the best of him (slanting his objectivity), this long out of print work gives many valuable bits of information concerning the development of all branches of Louisiana Masonry. The Introduction, by Alain Bernheim, and the Afterword, by Michael R. Poll, are themselves significant Masonic historical works which add greatly to the collected knowledge of early Louisiana Masonry.

The Grand Orient of Louisiana
A Short History and Catechism of a Lost
French Rite Masonic Body
Introduction by Michael R. Poll
Softcover 52 pages
Retail Price: $14.95
ISBN 1-934935-23-9

An amazing look into a forgotten Masonic body existing in New Orleans during the late 1800's and early 1900's. The Grand Orient of Louisiana was created to accommodate those working in the French Rite of Freemasonry in Louisiana. This rare work offers important information on the organizational structure and catechism of this unique Louisiana Masonic body. This is in indispensable book for any student of Freemasonry.

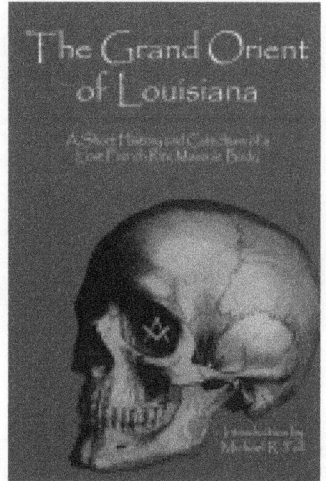

The Schism Between
the Scotch & York Rites
by Charles Laffon de Ladébat
6x9 Softcover 66 pages
Retail Price: $14.95
ISBN 1-934935-33-6

In 1850, everything changed for Louisiana Freemasons. Gone was the European style of Freemasonry as practiced by the Grand Lodge of Louisiana since its creation. By force, Louisiana was made to conform to the style of Masonry used by the rest of the U.S. Grand Lodges. This 1853 publication by Charles Laffon de Ladebat shows the emotion, frustration, confusion and pain experienced by the Creole New Orleans Masons as a result of the Masonic "war" that was inflicted upon them.

Lectures of the Ancient and Primitive Rite of Freemasonry
by John Yarker
6x9 Softcover 218 pages
Retail Price: $18.95
ISBN 1-934935-10-7

Lectures
of the
Ancient and Primitive Rite
of Freemasonry

by John Yarker

John Yarker provides a valuable resource for the lectures and catechisms of the Ancient and Primitive Rite of Freemasonry. Lectures of the Chapter, Senate, and Council, according to the forms of the Ancient and Primitive Rite, but embracing all Systems of High Grade Masonry.

Our Stations and Places - Masonic Officer's Handbook
by Henry G. Meacham
Revised by Michael R. Poll
Softcover 164 pages
Retail Price: $16.95
ISBN 1-887560-63-7

Our Stations
And Places

Masonic Officer's Handbook

Revised Edition

by Henry G. Meacham
Revised by Michael R. Poll

One of the most respected Masonic officer's handbooks has been revised for the 21st century Freemason. The various stations of the lodge are examined and practical suggestions are offered to help each officer best perform his duties. This revised and updated edition has been expanded to include a new section for the various lodge committees. This is an indispensable tool for all Lodge officers.

"If it was up to me every lodge should have a collection of these books on hand for every officer to read before the installation so he is well aware of what is expected of him in the upcoming year."
Cory Sigler, *The Working Tools Magazine*

Robert's Rules of Order: Masonic Edition
Revised by Michael R. Poll
Softcover 212 pages
Retail Price: $17.95
ISBN 1-887560-07-6

A Masonic bestseller!

Experienced legislators, editors, civic leaders, business executives, and club officers all pronounce Roberts Rules of Order the best parliamentary Guide in the English language. Its amazing acceptance entitles it to the claim of being the recognized authority in parliamentary law. Now, for the first time, the most comprehensive, understandable, and logical guide to smooth-running meetings has been revised for use in Masonic lodges and appendant bodies.

This is a must for every Masonic lodge officer.

"I strongly recommend this book to all Worshipful Masters, and those who will be in that position, and those who have been but are still interested in helping their Worshipful Masters." -Paul M. Bessel, Past Senior Grand Warden of the Grand Lodge of Washington DC

"I have used W. Bro. Michael's Masonic edition with much success in guiding the affairs of Masonic organizations. I have also used the Masonic edition to mediate disputes. I have even used the Masonic edition in a legal/evidentiary context in court proceedings. While W. Bro. Michael's Masonic edition of Robert's Rules of Order is not binding law in many Masonic jurisdictions, the Masonic edition of the Rules is a helpful guide for the efficient administration and governance of a fraternal organization.

The Masonic edition of the Robert's Rules of Order is an excellent tool for any Masonic organization. I recommend it to every Masonic organization that enjoys peace and harmony in the governance of Masonic affairs."
-Marc Conrad, PM, Asst. Grand Attorney, Grand Lodge of Louisiana, F&AM

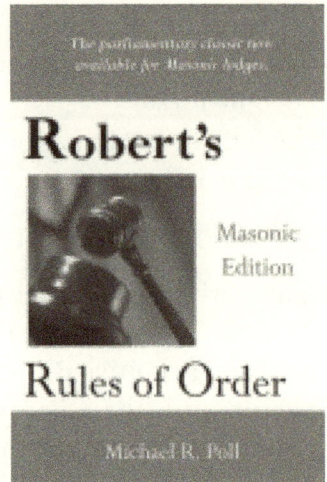

Masonic Words and Phrases
Edited by Michael R. Poll
Softcover 116 pages
Retail Price: $12.95
ISBN 1-887560-11-4

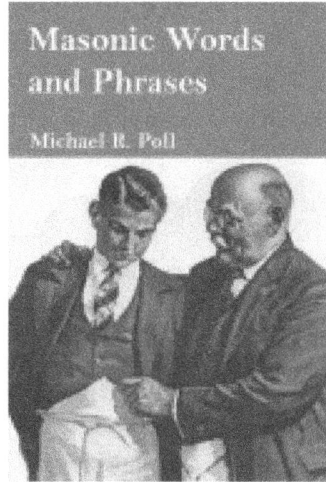

Masonic Words
and Phrases

Michael R. Poll

New Masons quickly learn that many unfamiliar words and phrases are employed in our symbolic teachings. Our words are not haphazardly selected, but have deep symbolic and historic significance.

Masonic Word and Phrases is a wonderful collection of the most often used words and phrases in Masonry. Presented in an easy to read and understandable format, this work provides any student of Masonry with a clear understanding of the meaning of our many phrases and words so seldom used outside of Masonry.

This work is valuable to the experienced Mason as a quick and handy reference guide. For the new Mason, however, it is an indispensable work and one that should augment any Masonic education program.

Review

"Many of the words and phrases used in Masonry were borrowed from the craft guilds, from other languages, or from the philosophical vocabularies of the day. This book (which makes a fine companion book to "Masonic Questions and Answers," shown above, provides brief but clear explanations of many of the terms used in Masonic tradition and ritual. Often, Brother Poll goes beyond a surface meaning to show the history of the word, which makes it a richer experience. For an example, consider the entry for "Token." This is from the Greek "deigma," meaning "example" or "proof" - the origin of the word "teach", and in its original sense had much the same meaning as sign or symbol, for it was an object used as a sign of something else. It is generally used, however, in the sense of a pledge or of an object which proves something. In our usage, a token is something that exhibits, or shows, or proves that we are Masons the grip of recognition, for example.

This is one of those basic books that belongs in every Lodge library."

- Jim Tresner, Book Review Editor, *The Scottish Rite Journal*

Masonic Enlightenment
The Philosophy, History and
Wisdom of Freemasonry
Edited by Michael R. Poll
6x9 Softcover 180 pages
Retail Price: $18.95
ISBN 1-887560-75-0

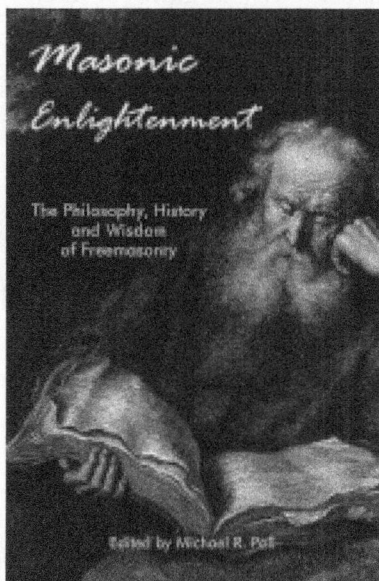

A Masonic Bestseller

A Masonic education from the first page to last. Includes: "The Meaning of Initiation" by Frank C. Higgins; "Operative Masonry: Early Days in the Masonic Era" by Robert I. Clegg; "Masonic Jurisprudence" by Roscoe Pound; "Freemasons in the American Revolution" by Charles S. Lobingier; "A Bird's-Eye View of Masonic History" by H.L. Haywood; "Women and Freemasonry" by Dudley Wright; "In the Interests of the Brethren" by Rudyard Kipling; "The Egyptian Influence on Our Masonic Ceremonial and Ritual" by Thomas Ross; "Anderson's Constitutions of 1723" by Lionel Vibert; "The Rise and Development of Anti-Masonry in America, 1737-1826" by J. Hugo Tatsch; "The Spiritual Significance of Freemasonry" by Silas H. Shepherd; "Rosicrucianism in Freemasonry" by H.V.B. Voorhis; "The New Atlantis and Freemasonry" by A.J.B. Milborne; "Masonry and World Peace" by Joseph Fort Newton and more.

Review

Mike Poll has pulled together a variety of essays from past generations and presented them for the enlightenment of Masons today. These are time-tested thoughts and ideas which older members may have encountered decades ago but which newer members may have never seen. Regardless of your Masonic age, you'll find this small book a delight to read. Whether you devour it on a snowy evening or read a single essay while waiting for car repair to finish, you'll find it a perfect companion and WELL worth the price.
- Edward L. King

The Secret Tradition in Freemasonry
by A. E. Waite
2 volumes 6x9 Softcover 926 pages
Retail Price: $69.95
Website Price: $56.95
ISBN 1-934935-13-1

Many say that this 1911 classic two volume set is the most significant work on the esoteric nature of Freemasonry ever written. Waite provides a detailed account of craft Masonry along with the many allied and high grade bodies along with a study of the symbolism and nature of the various rites.

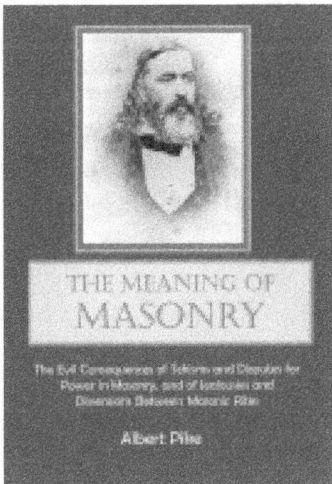

The Meaning of Masonry
by Albert Pike
6x9 Softcover 56 pages
Retail Price: $12.95
ISBN 1-887560-20-3

A biting lecture read at the request of the Grand Lodge of Louisiana, by Albert Pike in 1858. The lecture was subtitled, "The Evil Consequences of Schisms and Disputes for Power in Masonry, and of Jealousies and Dissensions Between Masonic Rites" and is a fascinating look at Pike's interpretation of the "Masonic wars" of the mid 1800's in Louisiana.

Morals and Dogma of the Scottish Rite Craft Degrees
by Albert Pike
Foreword by Michael R. Poll
6x9 Softcover 152 pages
Retail Price: $14.95
ISBN 1-887560-86-6

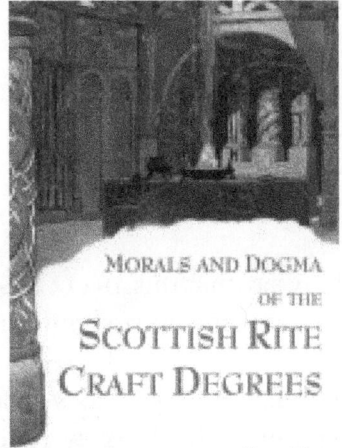

MORALS AND DOGMA
OF THE
SCOTTISH RITE
CRAFT DEGREES

Albert Pike

The philosophy of the Entered Apprentice, Fellowcraft and Master Mason degrees of the Ancient and Accepted Scottish Rite are explored, analyzed and interpreted in this work by Albert Pike. The AASR student will find much food for thought in this craft lodge section from Pike's classic "Morals and Dogma." A valuable and inspired work.

The Lodge of Perfection
by Albert Pike
Foreword by Michael R. Poll
6x9 Softcover 152 pages
Retail Price: $16.95
ISBN 1-934935-13-1

The degrees of the Lodge of Perfection are often viewed as the heart of the Scottish Rite. In these degrees, Albert Pike explores human relations, responsibilities and moral codes. We learn of how humans should interact with each other, how we should govern ourselves and live within our communities. "The Lodge of Perfection" provides each Masonic student with a collection of reflective philosophical lessons which can be used to grow as both a Mason and a member of the human family. The text has been somewhat modernized making an easier reading experience.

www.ingramcontent.com/pod-product-compliance
Lightning Source LLC
Chambersburg PA
CBHW032020090426

42741CB00006B/668